# BOND YIELD ANALYSIS

*A Guide to Predicting Bond Returns*

**Stuart R. Veale**

NEW YORK INSTITUTE OF FINANCE

*Library of Congress Cataloging-in-Publication Data*

Veale, Stuart R.
  Bond Yield Analysis

  Includes index.
  1. Bonds—United States. I. Title.
  HG4963.V43  1986      332.63'23      87–11305
  ISBN  0–13–079674–3

This publication is designed to provide accurate and authoritative information in regard to the subject matter covered. It is sold with the understanding that the publisher is not engaged in rendering legal, accounting, or other professional service. If legal advice or other expert  assistance is required, the services of a competent professional person should be sought.

*—From a Declaration of Principles Jointly Adopted by a Committee of the American Bar Association and a Committee of Publishers and Associations*

© **1988 by NYIF Corp.**
A Division of Simon & Schuster, Inc.
70 Pine Street
New York, New York 10270-0003

Printed in the United States of America
10  9  8  7  6  5  4  3  2  1

New York Institute of Finance
(NYIF Corp.)
70 Pine Street
New York, NY 10270-0003

# CONTENTS

# LIST OF TABLES

# INTRODUCTION

Many investors still consider bonds to be a stodgy investment. This is unfortunate because the bond market is actually a very dynamic and diverse market, in which investors can select an investment vehicle and/or strategy that's right for them in light of their objectives and circumstances. Both the most conservative retiree and the most aggressive speculator can find appropriate investment vehicles and strategies in the bond market.

The trick, of course, is to match the right investment strategy with the right investor. This has become more difficult recently for two principal reasons. First, there has been a proliferation of new types of debt instruments. These new instruments, while providing greater flexibility for both issuers and investors, do tend to "complicate" the bond market and thereby confuse bond investors. Second, the increased volatility of interest rates has, in turn, increased the volatility of bond prices, making the "timing" of bond purchases and sales more difficult.

Because of these changes, now more than ever before it is essential for bond investors to have a thorough understanding of the factors that impact upon bond prices and bond yields, and to understand how these factors interact. This book was written to provide investors, stockbrokers, financial planners, and other professionals with a basic understanding of how to calculate bond yields and how to analyze the potential return of a specific bond investment.

I hope that after reading this text you will have a greater understanding of the different components that make up the total return of a debt instrument, and further realize that different debt instruments are nothing more than these same components combined in different ways.

# Chapter 1

# Quoting Bond Market Prices

Different types of debt instruments have their market prices quoted by different conventions. It's important to use the right convention with the right instrument.

## Corporate Bonds

Corporate bonds with longer than one year to maturity are generally quoted as a percentage of their face value to the nearest eighth. Thus a price of a given bond might be

$$109^3/_8 \quad 92^7/_8 \quad 112^1/_2 \quad 56^1/_4$$

Converting these quotes into dollar prices gives us:

$109^3/_8 = 109^3/_8\%$ of \$1000 or = \$1090 + \$3.75 = \$1093.75

$92^7/_8 = 92^7/_8\%$ of \$1000 or = \$ 920 + \$8.75 = \$ 928.75

$112^1/_2 = 112^1/_2\%$ of \$1000 or = \$1120 + \$5.00 = \$1125.00

$56^1/_4 = 56^1/_4\%$ of \$1000 or = \$ 560 + \$2.50 = \$ 562.50

Thus a dealer with a half-point spread between the bid price and ask price for a corporate bond might quote the bond as 109³/₈–109⁷/₈.

Corporate bonds with less than one year to maturity are quoted by sixteenths instead of eighths. Thus a corporate bond with less than a year to maturity might be quoted as 98¹³/₁₆–98¹⁴/₁₆.

An alternative way for dealers to quote bonds to investors and to other dealers is to quote the bond's *yield*. Thus a dealer might quote a bond as 9.45% by 9.5%. This means that the dealer will buy the bond at whatever price it takes to yield the dealer 9.5% and will sell the bond to prospective purchasers at whatever price will give the investor a yield of 9.45%. Thus the dealer's *markup*, or *spread*, is 0.05%, or 5 *basis points* (a basis point being 1/100 of a percent).

One of the topics covered in this book is how to determine a bond's dollar price given its yield and vice versa.

## U.S. Government Notes and Bonds

U.S. government notes and bonds are also quoted on a percentage basis but to the nearest 1/32 percent instead of to the nearest 1/8 or 1/16 percent. This is because the market for government bonds is more liquid than the market for corporates and the spread between the bid price and asked price is often narrower.

Some examples of price quotes for U.S. government bonds are

$$68.22 \quad 98.30 \quad 104.01 \quad 124.16$$

Converting these quotes into prices would give us:

$$
\begin{aligned}
68.22 &= 68.22\% \text{ of } \$1000 = \$\ 680 + \$6.875 = \$\ 686.88 \\
98.30 &= 98.30\% \text{ of } \$1000 = \$\ 980 + \$9.375 = \$\ 989.38 \\
104.01 &= 104.01\% \text{ of } \$1000 = \$1040 + \$0.313 = \$1040.31 \\
124.16 &= 124.16\% \text{ of } \$1000 = \$1240 = 45.000 = \$1245.00
\end{aligned}
$$

Thus a dealer quote with a spread of 1/32 percent between the bid and asked price might be

$$68.22\text{–}66.23 \quad 124.16\text{–}124.17$$

These notes and bonds are also quoted on a yield basis.

## Simple Interest

*Simple interest* is the "rent" a borrower pays to an investor for the use of the investor's money. For example, if an investor lends the IBM\* corporation $1000 for 5 years at the simple interest rate of 5%, the investor would receive $50 per year from IBM for the use of the investor's $1000. Over the 5-year term of the loan, the investor would be entitled to 5 x 50 or $250. The formula for calculating simple interest is

Simple Interest (SI) = (P)rincipal x (R)ate x (T)ime
SI = $1000 x 0.05 x 5 = $250

The total number of dollars due the investor over the term of a simple-interest investment is equal to:

Total Dollars Returned (TDR) = P + (P x R x T)
= $1000 + ($1000 x 0.05 x 5) = $1250

If we assume that the rent (interest) is paid to the investor on a semiannual basis and that the principal is returned to the investor in one lump sum at the conclusion of the 5-year period, then a cash-flow summary of the above loan would look like Table 1-1 (see page 4).

As you can see from Table 1-1, the "amount invested" with a simple-interest loan is always the same. Also, the investor receives the same amount every 6 months until the loan's maturity date, at which time the principal is also returned. Thus the formula for calculating simple interest assumes that the interest received is *not* reinvested.

The only time a simple-interest analysis and cash-flow summary can be used to reflect accurately what happens with a loan is when the borrower is spending the interest as soon as it is received (as in the case of a retiree who uses 100% of his interest payments to meet his current living expenses). Of course this is very rarely the case.

---

\* IBM is a registered trademark of International Business Machines Corporation.

**Table 1-1.** Cash Flow for a 5-Year, 10% Simple-Interest Loan (Semiannual Interest Compounding).

| Period | Time | Amount Invested | Funds Received per Period | Accumulated Funds Received |
|---|---|---|---|---|
| 1 | 6 months | $1000 | $ 25 | $ 25 |
| 2 | 1 year | 1000 | 25 | 50 |
| 3 | 18 months | 1000 | 25 | 75 |
| 4 | 2 years | 1000 | 25 | 100 |
| 5 | 30 months | 1000 | 25 | 125 |
| 6 | 3 years | 1000 | 25 | 150 |
| 7 | 42 months | 1000 | 25 | 175 |
| 8 | 4 years | 1000 | 25 | 200 |
| 9 | 64 months | 1000 | 25 | 225 |
| 10 | 5 years | 1000 | 1025 | 1250 |

## Compound Interest

Usually, investors of all ages *reinvest* at least a portion of the interest payments they receive as they receive them. Thus investors usually receive interest not only on their original investment but also on the interest payments they receive and then reinvest. Let's examine what happens to the loan described above if we make the assumption that each of the interest payments received is reinvested at the same 5% interest rate at which the original loan amount was invested. When the interest is reinvested in this manner, the interest is said to be *compounding*.

It's important to note that the overall time frame of the investment remains 5 years. Thus we assume that we are going to reinvest the first interest payment we receive for a term of $4^1/2$ years, the second interest payment for a period of 4 years, and so on. Thus we assume that all of our reinvestments will mature on the same *date* as the original investment's maturity date.

If the interest from the bond described above is allowed to compound, then, in the second time period, there is no longer just $1000 invested at 5%, but, instead, $1025. This is equal to the $1000 original principal plus the first $25 interest payment.

**Table 1-2.** *Cash Flow for a 5-Year, 10% Loan Where the Interest Is Reinvested as It Is Received (Compounded Interest).*

| Period | Time | Amount Invested | Funds Received per Period | Accumulated Funds |
|--------|------|-----------------|--------------------------|-------------------|
| 1 | 6 months | $1000.00 | $ 25.00 | $1025.00 |
| 2 | 1 year | 1025.00 | 25.63 | 1050.63 |
| 3 | 18 months | 1050.63 | 26.26 | 1076.89 |
| 4 | 2 years | 1076.89 | 26.92 | 1103.81 |
| 5 | 30 months | 1103.81 | 27.60 | 1131.41 |
| 6 | 3 years | 1131.41 | 28.28 | 1159.69 |
| 7 | 42 months | 1159.69 | 29.00 | 1188.69 |
| 8 | 4 years | 1188.69 | 29.71 | 1218.40 |
| 9 | 64 months | 1218.40 | 30.46 | 1248.86 |
| 10 | 5 years | 1248.86 | 1031.22 | 1280.08 |

During the third time period, the amount invested rises to $1050.63. The composition of this amount is the $1000 original principal plus two $25 simple-interest payments on that principal plus $0.63 of interest earned by reinvesting the first $25 interest payment during the second 6-month period. Thus a cash-flow summary for the above bond (assuming that the interest is allowed to compound) would look like Table 1-2 above.

As we can see from this table, when the interest is allowed to compound, the amount invested increases as time passes. Also, the total number of dollars accumulated over a given time period is larger when the interest payments received are reinvested. The difference between the number of dollars accumulated via simple interest and via compound interest (assuming all other factors are equal) is equal to the amount of interest earned on reinvested interest payments. We will call interest earned this way *interest on interest (IOI)*.

For *any investment* that's allowed to compound, the total number of dollars returned *(TDR)* to the investor over the time period is equal to:

(P)rincipal + (I)nterest + (I)nterest (O)n (I)nterest

So the TDR for a compounding investment is equal to:

$$TDR = P + I + IOI$$

If we assume that the interest payments are *reinvested at the same interest rate* as the original investment, then there is a second formula that we can use to determine the TDR of a compounding investment. This formula is

$$TDR = P \times (1 + i)^n$$

where $i$ = interest rate per period
        $n$ = number of compounding periods
For the example above:

$$TDR = \$1000 \times (1 + 0.025)^{10} = \$1280.08$$

To find the *interest component (IC)* of the loan, we use the formula:

$$TDR - P = IC$$
$$\$1280.08 - \$1000 = \$280.08$$

The IOI component is then equal to IC minus the simple interest.

$$IC - SI = IOI$$
$$\$280.08 - \$250 = \$30.08$$

Thus the difference in total number of dollars earned by the investor in a simple-interest investment as opposed to a compound-interest investment is $30.08. This $30.08 represents the interest on interest (IOI) that the investor earns by reinvesting the interest payments as they are received at the same interest rate as the original investment.

Expressed as a percentage, the IOI component of this example is

$$\frac{IOI}{IC} \times 100 = \% \text{ of Total Interest} \qquad \frac{\$30.08}{\$280.08} \times 100 = 10.74\%$$

$$\frac{IOI}{TDR} \times 100 = \% \text{ of Total Dollar Return} \qquad \frac{\$30.08}{\$1280.08} \times 100 = 2.35\%$$

Thus for the above example, the IOI component makes up 10.74% of the interest received and 2.35% of the total dollars returned.

## Factors Which Determine the Relative Size of the Three Components Which Make Up a Loan's TDR

There are three principal variables that affect the relative contribution that the IOI component makes to a loan's TDR: the time horizon, the interest rate, and the frequency with which the interest is compounded. Let's turn our attention now to the relationship between these variables and the percentage of a loan's TDR that's contributed by IOI.

### The Relationship Between the Time Horizon and the IOI Component

The longer the term of a loan, the more time there is for the simple interest that the investor receives to be reinvested. The longer the term over which the interest can be reinvested, the more IOI it will earn. Logically, then, we would expect that *the longer the time horizon of the loan, the larger the percentage of the loan's TDR that will be contributed by the IOI component* (assuming, of course, that all other factors remain constant).

Indeed, as Table 1-3 (see page 8) shows, by lengthening the term of the loan, we increase the percentage of the TDR that will be contributed by IOI.

Thus we can see that as the time frame we consider increases, the contribution of IOI to TDR increases on both an absolute and a relative basis.

***Table 1-3.*** *The Effect of Lengthening the Time Horizon on the Relative Contribution of the Various Components to the TDR of a Loan ($1000 Loan Compounded Semiannually for 5 Years).*

| No. of Years | TDR | P | SI | IOI | IOI as a % of TDR |
|---|---|---|---|---|---|
| 1 | $1050.63 | $1000 | $ 50 | $ 0.63 | 0.06 |
| 5 | 1280.08 | 1000 | 250 | 30.08 | 2.35 |
| 10 | 1638.62 | 1000 | 500 | 138.62 | 8.46 |
| 15 | 2097.57 | 1000 | 750 | 347.57 | 16.57 |
| 20 | 2685.06 | 1000 | 1000 | 685.06 | 25.51 |
| 25 | 3437.11 | 1000 | 1250 | 1187.11 | 34.54 |
| 30 | 4399.79 | 1000 | 1500 | 1899.79 | 43.18 |

## The Relationship Between the Interest Rate and the IOI Component

The higher the interest rate, the more interest the investor receives. The more interest the investor receives, the more interest available to be reinvested. The more interest available to be reinvested, the greater the amount of IOI. The greater the amount of IOI, the greater the IOI component should be relative to the other two components (again, assuming that all other factors remain constant).

Indeed, as Table 1-4 (see page 9) shows, by increasing the interest rate that our investment earns, we increase the percentage of the TDR that's contributed by IOI.

Thus we can see that as the interest rate increases, the contribution of IOI to TDR on both an absolute and a relative basis also increases.

## The Relationship Between the Frequency of Compounding and the IOI Component

As we increase the frequency of compounding, we decrease the amount of time that passes before our interest starts earning IOI. The sooner our interest starts earning additional interest, the more IOI we will earn and the greater the IOI component will be (again, assuming that all other factors remain constant.)

**Table 1-4.** The Effect of Increasing the Interest Rate on the Relative Contribution of the Various Components to the TDR of a Loan ($1000 Loan Compounded Semiannually for 5 Years).

| Interest Rate | TDR | P | SI | IOI | IOI as a % of TDR |
|---|---|---|---|---|---|
| 01.0% | $1051.14 | $1000 | $ 50 | $ 1.14 | 0.11 |
| 05.0% | 1280.08 | 1000 | 250 | 30.08 | 2.35 |
| 07.5% | 1445.04 | 1000 | 375 | 70.04 | 4.85 |
| 10.0% | 1628.89 | 1000 | 500 | 128.89 | 7.91 |
| 12.5% | 1833.54 | 1000 | 625 | 208.54 | 11.37 |
| 15.0% | 2061.03 | 1000 | 750 | 311.03 | 15.09 |

**Table 1-5.** The Periodic Interest Rate for Different Compounding Periods.

| Compounding Frequency | No. of Compounding Periods | Interest Rate per Period |
|---|---|---|
| Annual | 5 | 5.000 |
| Semiannual | 10 | 2.500 |
| Quarterly | 20 | 1.250 |
| Monthly | 60 | 0.417 |
| Daily | 1800 | 0.014 |

**Table 1-6.** The Effect of Increasing the Frequency of Compounding on the Relative Contribution of the Various Components to the TDR of a Loan ($1000 Loan Compounded at Various Frequencies at a 5% Interest Rate over a 5-Year Time Period).

| Frequency | TDR | P | SI | IOI | IOI as a % of TDR |
|---|---|---|---|---|---|
| Annual | $1276.28 | $1000 | $250 | $26.28 | 2.06 |
| Semiannual | 1280.08 | 1000 | 250 | 30.08 | 2.35 |
| Quarterly | 1282.04 | 1000 | 250 | 32.04 | 2.50 |
| Monthly | 1283.36 | 1000 | 250 | 33.59 | 2.62 |
| Daily | 1284.00 | 1000 | 250 | 34.00 | 2.65 |

Indeed, as Tables 1-5 and 1-6 (see page 9) show, by increasing the frequency at which our investment compounds, we increase the percentage of the TDR that's contributed by IOI.

Thus we can see that as the frequency of compounding increases, the contribution of IOI to TDR on both an absolute and a relative basis also increases.

## Chapter 2

# *Introduction to Bonds*

A *bond* is a security which represents a loan from an investor to the issuer. The "rent" for the use of this money is the interest the issuer (or borrower) pays to the bondholder (or investor). Since bonds are loans, you might reasonably expect that you could use the compound interest formula:

$$\text{TDR} = P \times (1 + i)^n$$

discussed in the last chapter to compute the total dollar return from a bond investment.

Unfortunately, bond calculations are not that simple (otherwise this would be the last page of this book). The reason you cannot use the compound-interest formula is that in order for this simple formula to be valid, certain assumptions must be made.

These assumptions are

1. Both the principal and interest will be paid in full and on time.

(In other words, the formula is not sufficiently flexible to accommodate delayed or missed payments of principal and/or interest.)

2. The principal will be returned in one lump sum at the conclusion of the loan period. (In other words, the formula cannot accommodate either periodic and/or sporadic returns of principal prior to the bond's scheduled maturity.)

3. The time frame of the investment (i.e., the maturity of the bond) is known exactly. (In other words, the formula cannot accommodate either the issuer or the investor terminating the investment prior to its scheduled maturity.)

4. The amount invested is equal to the principal value. (In other words, the formula is invalid for bonds that are purchased at a price that is lower than their face amount, i.e., at a discount, or higher than their face amount, i.e., at a premium.)

5. The interest rate received on the original principal will stay constant over the term of the investment. (In other words, the formula makes no provision for the possibility that the interest rate we earn on our principal will change, or *float*, over the time period of the investment.)

6. We will be able to reinvest the interest payments received at the same yield as the original investment. (In other words, the formula is invalid unless the reinvestment rate for each coupon payment the investor receives is the same as the yield of the original investment.)

7. The interest payments will be made on a regular schedule, i.e., every 6 months. (Irregular interest payments invalidate the formula.)

8. The purchase settles on an interest payment date. (In other words, the formula makes no provision for the effect that "accrued interest" can have on the TDR.)

All in all, these are some very *big* assumptions—and assumptions that almost always make it impossible to apply the compound-interest formula discussed in the last chapter.

Consider the following:

The first assumption, timely payment of principal and interest, is not always true. While most bonds pay their interest and principal "in full and on time," every year a certain percentage of the bonds outstanding either make their interest payments late or simply go into permanent default. The risk of this happening is called *credit risk*, and, in order for us to analyze bond yields accurately, we must make some provision for this risk.

The second assumption, that the principal will be returned in one lump sum at maturity, is not true for mortgage pass-through securities. This class of securities includes Ginnie Maes, Fannie Maes, Freddie Macs, and so on. Therefore, in order for our analysis to be correct, we must make provision for both periodic and sporadic returns of principal in our analysis.

The third assumption, that neither the borrower nor the investor can alter the bond's maturity, is not valid because many bonds have call provisions or put provisions. *Call provisions* allow the issuer to shorten the time frame of the bond, and *put provisions* allow the investor to shorten the time frame of the bond. Therefore, our analysis must also take these provisions into account if it is going to be valid.

The fourth assumption, that the bond is purchased for an amount equal to its face or maturity value, is also not valid. Most bonds are purchased for less than or more than their maturity value. Our analysis therefore must also take this into account if it is going to be valid.

The fifth assumption, that the interest rate earned by the principal will stay constant, or fixed, while true in many cases, is certainly false for floating-rate securities and adjustable-rate securities. Thus our analysis must make provision for changing interest rates.

The sixth assumption, that we will be able to reinvest the coupons at the same interest rate, is almost ludicrous. Interest rates change constantly, and therefore our reinvestment rate will also vary from reinvestment to reinvestment. Also, as we receive the progressively later interest payments, we reinvest them for progressively shorter terms and thus usually at progressively lower yields. Therefore, our reinvestment rate will change unless all bonds with the same credit rating offer the same yield regardless of maturity. Our analysis will have to accommodate changing reinvestment rates if it is going to be valid.

The seventh assumption, that all interest payments will be made on a regular schedule (either monthly, quarterly, or semiannually), is not valid because many bonds (including many mortgage securities and municipal bonds) are issued with irregular first coupons. Also, many trades occur with irregular settlement dates that must be taken into account.

The eighth assumption, that all bond trades settle on an interest payment date, is also ridiculous. There are over 250 business days in a year and, therefore, over 250 potential settlement days. Since most bonds have only two payment dates, the vast majority of settlements will not occur on an interest payment date.

Since the formula for compound interest is not valid when analyzing bonds, we need to develop a different method, one that is more flexible and that will be valid in light of these complications.

In order to develop a valid analytical method, let's first explore how the different bond variables—face value, purchase price, coupon size, and assumed reinvestment rate(s)—interact to determine the TDR and yield(s) of a given bond. Once we do this, we'll be able to explore how the premature return of principal, changing interest rates, accrued interest, irregular periodic payments, and changing credit quality also affect a given bond's TDR.

## Bond Yields

Before we can analyze how these factors affect a given bond's yield, we have to settle on a definition of *yield* because the term means different things to different investors. Most bonds have many yields, including coupon yield, current yield, yield to maturity, yield to call, yield to put, realized compound yield, net realized compound yield, and net-net realized compound yield. For a given bond, the above yields can all be the same or, more commonly, can all be different. Also, as we shall see, different investors with different investment objectives are interested in different yields.

Let's examine each of these different yields.

## Nominal or Coupon Yield

The *nominal yield (NY)* , or *coupon yield,* is the number of dollars of interest paid to an investor over a one-year time period divided by the bond's *face* or *maturity value,* expressed as a percentage. Thus, if a bond has a face value of $1000 and paid the investor $60 a year in interest, the nominal yield would be ($60/$1000) x 100, or 6%. If a bond with a $5000 maturity value paid investors $450 of interest per year, the nominal yield would be ($450/$5000) x 100, or 9%.

The coupon yield, or nominal yield, is usually printed right on the bond certificate. The nominal yield of a bond never changes unless the bond is a floating-rate security.

## Current Yield

The *current yield (CY)* is the number of dollars of interest paid to an investor over a one-year period divided by the bond's *market value,* expressed as a percentage. Most bonds are purchased for prices that differ from their face amounts. (The reasons for this are the subjects of several later chapters.) Since bonds' market values change constantly, so do bonds' current yields.

Thus, if the bonds described above were purchased for $1200 and $4700 respectively, the current yields would be ($60/$1200) x 100, or 5%, and ($450/$4700) x 100, or 9.57%. If, at some later time, the market value of these bonds was to change to $1100 and $4900, respectively, then their current yields would also change to ($60/$1100) x 100, or 5.45%, and ($450/$4900) x 100, or 9.18%.

The current yield is often the most important yield to an investor who does not plan to reinvest the interest payments. For example, if a retiree was going to invest his lump-sum pension distribution with the principal objective of providing himself with an income to live on in his retirement years, he would be most interested in how many dollars of interest his nest egg will generate per year.

## Yield to Maturity

The *yield to maturity (YTM)* recognizes that an investor who purchases a bond at a price that is different from the bond's face value will experience a gain or a loss if the bond is held until its maturity date. Using the examples above, if the first bond is purchased for $1200, then the investor will experience a $200 loss when the bond matures and pays the investor its face value of $1000. If the second bond is purchased for $4700, then the investor will experience a $300 gain when the bond matures and pays the investor its face amount of $5000.

Of course, in the real world, the investor does not experience this gain or loss all at once; rather the gain or loss is *prorated* (added to or subtracted from the bond's market value) over the remaining life of the bond.

When this prorated gain or loss is added to (or subtracted from) the bond's coupon payment and that total is then divided by the number of dollars invested, the result is an approximation of the bond's yield to maturity (we'll give a more exact definition a little later). Expressing the above as a formula gives us:

$$\text{YTM} = \frac{\text{(Interest received per year} \pm \text{prorated gain or loss)}}{\text{Average number of dollars invested over term of bond}} \times 100$$

The first component of this equation, the interest received per year is, in most cases, a known value.

To get a rough approximation of the prorated gain or loss, divide the total gain or loss that the investor will experience if the bond is held to its maturity by the time remaining until the bond matures.

The average number of dollars invested can be approximated by averaging the purchase price of the bond and the maturity value of the bond. The reasoning that supports making this approximation is as follows:

On the day the bond matures, the bond is "worth" its maturity value. On the day the bond is purchased, it is "worth" the purchase

**Figure 2-1.** *The Amortization of a Premium Bond and a Discount Bond.*

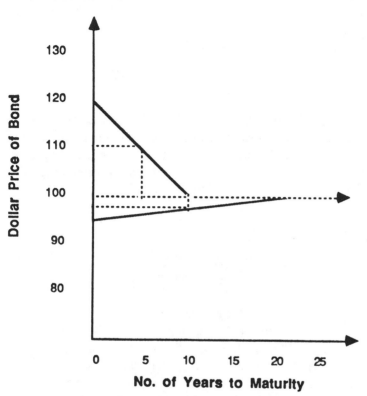

price (at least to its purchaser). Every day from the day the bond is purchased until the bond matures, the bond's value moves toward the bond's maturity value and away from the bond's purchase price. Over time, then, the "worth" of the bond (and thus the number of dollars the investor has tied up in the bond) moves away from the bond's purchase price and toward the bond's maturity value (see Figure 2-1 above).

It stands to reason, therefore, that the average number of dollars the investor has tied up in the bond over the life of the bond is the *halfway point* between the bond's purchase price and the bond's maturity value.

If we assume that the first bond illustrated above matures in 10 years and that the second bond illustrated above matures in 20 years, then the calculation to approximate the bonds' YTM would be:

First bond's YTM $= \dfrac{\$60 - (\$200/10)}{(\$1200 + \$1000)/2}$

$= \dfrac{\$60 - \$20}{\$1100} = \dfrac{\$40}{\$1100} = 3.64\%$

For the second bond, it is easier to first adjust all of the values to reflect their value per thousand dollars of face amount before we put them into the formula. In this case, that means dividing the purchase price, the maturity value, the interest earned, and the prorated gain by 5 before plugging those variables into the equation.

Second bond's YTM $= \dfrac{\$90 + (\$60/20)}{(940 + \$1000)/2}$

$= \dfrac{\$90 + \$3}{\$970} = \dfrac{\$93}{\$970} = 9.59\%$

Not surprisingly, the YTM of the bond that we purchased at a premium to its face value is lower than that bond's current return (3.64% vs. 5%). This is because the prorated annual loss of principal, in effect, reduces the return generated by the bond's interest payments. However, the YTM of the bond that we purchased at a discount to its face value is higher than that bond's current yield (9.59% vs. 9.57%) because the bond's annual prorated appreciation supplements the bond's interest payments.

A slightly more cumbersome formula that yields a slightly more accurate estimate of a bond's YTM is a three-step process.

*Step 1*:

Interest income ± prorated gain or loss = Z

*Step 2:*

$$YTM = \cfrac{Z}{\text{Purchase price}}$$
$$+ \cfrac{Z}{\text{Maturity value} + \text{prorated loss} - \text{prorated gain}}$$

*Step 3:*

$$YTM = \frac{\text{Result of Step 2}}{2} \times 100$$

For the first bond, this calculation would be

*Step 1:*

$$\$60 - \$20 = \$40$$

*Step 2:*

$$\frac{\$40}{\$1200} + \frac{\$40}{(\$1000 + \$20)} = 0.0333 + 0.0392 = 0.0725$$

*Step 3:*

$$\frac{(0.0725)}{2} \times 100 = 3.626\%$$

For the second bond, the calculation would be

*Step 1:*

$$\$90 + \$3 = \$93$$

*Step 2:*

$$\frac{\$93}{\$940} + \frac{\$93}{(\$1000 - \$3)} = 0.0989 + 0.0933 = 0.1922$$

*Step 3*:

$$\frac{(0.1922)}{2} \times 100 = 9.61\%$$

These formulas only provide approximations of a bond's true YTM because they make several assumptions that are usually invalid.

First, these formulas assume that the bond's discount or premium is amortized in equal annual installments when, in fact, the discount or premium is actually accreted over the remaining life of the bond. This results in lower amortization in the early years and greater amortization in the years when the bond approaches maturity.

Second, these formulas assume that the number of dollars invested every year is equal to the average number of dollars invested over the holding period of the bond. In reality, however, the market value of the bond accretes from the purchase price to the maturity value over the term of the bond (assuming level market interest rates).

Third, just as with the compound-interest calculation in the last chapter, these formulas assume that each and every interest payment is reinvested at the same YTM as the YTM at which the bond was purchased. Thus, if the bond was purchased with a YTM of 9.61%, the assumption is made that every coupon payment received is also reinvested at a yield of 9.61%. The chances of reinvesting each and every coupon at the same YTM as the YTM of the bond when it was purchased are somewhere between extremely slim and none.

What does this mean about the usefulness of using YTM as a tool for analyzing bonds?

First, it means that *a bond's YTM is, at best, a very poor way to predict the total dollar return that the bond will actually generate for the investor*. At best, a YTM is a "guesstimate" (except in the case of zero-coupon bonds).

However, the fact that a bond's YTM does not provide information about a bond's total return on an "absolute" basis does not mean that the YTM is useless as an analytical tool. Indeed, YTM is very useful for comparing the relative attractiveness of one bond to another. As long as it is used to analyze the relative attractiveness of different bonds and not as a gauge of absolute return, YTM can be very valuable, as we shall see later.

To gauge a bond's "absolute" return over a given time period, we must acknowledge that each coupon will probably be reinvested at an interest rate different from the YTM at which the bond was originally purchased. Thus, when we try to anticipate a given bond's TDR, we can get a more accurate estimate if we use reinvestment rate assumptions that are more accurate than the bond's original YTM.

Of course, it's very difficult to predict future interest rates accurately. Therefore it's very difficult to predict future reinvestment rates for coupons. The science of predicting future interest rates is, at best, inexact. The further into the future you try to predict reinvestment rates, the less accurate your predictions are likely to be.

Despite the fact that no one has been able to predict future interest rates accurately over a long period of time (although an army of economists keeps trying), it is still better to use your "best guess" about future interest-rate levels than it is to assume that the reinvestment rate will be equal to the bond's original YTM.

The more accurate your predictions are regarding future interest rates, the more accurate your predictions of a given bond's TDR are going to be. Remember, however, that even if you calculate a bond's TDR by using your best estimates of future reinvestment rates, the result you get from your analysis is still just an estimate. You will never know the TDR return of a bond investment until after the bond has matured (except for zero-coupon bonds).

For example, assume that you buy a 15-year, 10% coupon bond at *par* (i.e., at its face value—$1000) that pays its interest semiannually. The YTM of this bond is 10%. If you expect, however, that soon after you acquire this bond, interest rates will drop to the 8% level and you're right, then you will get a much better estimate of the bond's TDR by assuming a reinvestment rate of 8%.

For the bond described above, we will compare the TDR for a 10% reinvestment assumption and an 8% reinvestment assumption. To do so, we prepare a cash-flow table similar to the one in the previous chapter, except that we design it so that it can take different reinvestment rates into account.

To do this, we examine each compounding period over the life of the bond separately. For each time period over the life of the bond, we take the coupon payment we receive and add to it the amount of

**Table 2-1.** Cash Flow for a 15-Year, 10% Bond
(Compounded Interest).

| Period | SI per Period | Total Interest | Cumulative SI | Cumulative IOI |
|--------|---------------|----------------|---------------|----------------|
| 1 | $50 + ( 0.0 x 1.05) = $ 50.00 | | $ 50 | $ 0.00 |
| 2 | 50 + ( 50.00 x 1.05) = 102.50 | | 100 | 2.50 |
| 3 | 50 + ( 102.50 x 1.05) = 157.62 | | 150 | 7.62 |
| 4 | 50 + ( 157.62 x 1.05) = 215.51 | | 200 | 15.51 |
| 5 | 50 + ( 215.51 x 1.05) = 276.29 | | 250 | 26.29 |
| 6 | 50 + ( 276.29 x 1.05) = 340.10 | | 300 | 40.10 |
| 7 | 50 + ( 340.10 x 1.05) = 407.10 | | 350 | 57.10 |
| 8 | 50 + ( 407.10 x 1.05) = 477.46 | | 400 | 77.46 |
| 9 | 50 + ( 477.46 x 1.05) = 551.33 | | 450 | 101.33 |
| 10 | 50 + ( 551.33 x 1.05) = 628.89 | | 500 | 128.89 |
| 11 | 50 + ( 628.89 x 1.05) = 710.34 | | 550 | 160.34 |
| 12 | 50 + ( 710.34 x 1.05) = 795.86 | | 600 | 195.86 |
| 13 | 50 + ( 795.86 x 1.05) = 885.65 | | 650 | 235.65 |
| 14 | 50 + ( 885.65 x 1.05) = 979.93 | | 700 | 279.93 |
| 15 | 50 + ( 979.93 x 1.05) = 1078.93 | | 750 | 328.93 |
| 16 | 50 + (1078.93 x 1.05) = 1182.87 | | 800 | 382.87 |
| 17 | 50 + (1182.87 x 1.05) = 1292.02 | | 850 | 442.02 |
| 18 | 50 + (1292.02 x 1.05) = 1406.62 | | 900 | 506.62 |
| 19 | 50 + (1406.62 x 1.05) = 1526.95 | | 950 | 576.95 |
| 20 | 50 + (1526.95 x 1.05) = 1653.30 | | 1000 | 653.30 |
| 21 | 50 + (1653.30 x 1.05) = 1785.96 | | 1050 | 745.96 |
| 22 | 50 + (1785.96 x 1.05) = 1925.26 | | 1100 | 825.26 |
| 23 | 50 + (1925.26 x 1.05) = 2071.52 | | 1150 | 921.52 |
| 24 | 50 + (2071.52 x 1.05) = 2225.10 | | 1200 | 1025.10 |
| 25 | 50 + (2225.10 x 1.05) = 2386.35 | | 1250 | 1136.35 |
| 26 | 50 + (2386.35 x 1.05) = 2555.67 | | 1300 | 1255.67 |
| 27 | 50 + (2555.67 x 1.05) = 2733.46 | | 1350 | 1383.46 |
| 28 | 50 + (2733.46 x 1.05) = 2920.13 | | 1400 | 1520.13 |
| 29 | 50 + (2920.13 x 1.05) = 3116.14 | | 1450 | 1666.14 |
| 30 | 50 + (3116.14 x 1.05) = 3321.94 | | 1500 | 1821.94 |

IOI we have already accumulated in order to compute the total interest received to that date. We then multiply that sum by our assumed reinvestment rate for the next compounding period.

Table 2-1 (opposite) shows the calculations for the bond described above.

If the total interest is $3321.94, then the TDR is equal to the total interest plus the principal, or $4321.94.

Because this example assumes that the reinvestment rate is the same as the interest rate at which the principal was originally invested, we can also use the compound-interest formula described in the previous chapter.

$$TDR = P \times (1 + i)^n$$
$$TDR = \$1000 \times (1 + 0.05)30 = \$4321.94$$

Thus the three components of TDR in this example are

$$
\begin{array}{rcl}
P & = & \$1000.00 \\
I & = & 1500.00 \\
IOI & = & \underline{1821.94} \\
& & \$4321.94
\end{array}
$$

Thus, the IOI component is the largest component (on both an absolute and on a percentage basis) of the bond's total TDR.

$$\frac{\$1821.94}{\$4321.94} \times 100 = 42.16\%$$

Unfortunately, the largest component is also the one we are the *least sure of* from the point of view of accuracy. If we do the same calculation but assume an 8% reinvestment rate, then we would expect that:

1. The bond will earn less IOI.
2. The TDR will be lower.
3. The percentage of the TDR that is contributed by the IOI component will decline.

To prove this, let's do the same calculation assuming an 8% reinvestment rate. (Note that because the yield at which the coupons are being reinvested is different from the bond's YTM at the time it was purchased, the compound interest formula *cannot* be used to do this calculation. For the time being, we have to use a cash-flow chart like the one in Table 2-2 (opposite) in order to solve this problem.)

Thus you can see that when the reinvestment rate is lowered to 8%, the bond's absolute return drops to $3887.50

| | |
|---|---|
| P component | $1000.00 |
| SI component | $1500.00 |
| IOI component | $1387.50 |
| | $3887.50 |

and the percentage of the absolute return that the IOI component contributes to TDR drops to:

$$\frac{\$1387.50}{\$3887.50} = 35.69\% \text{ of TDR}$$

### Realized Compound Yield

The one yield that will produce the TDR we will get from a bond if the reinvestment rate(s) is (are) *different* from the YTM is called the *realized compound yield (RCY)*. This term was first defined by Homer and Leibowitz in their book, *Inside the Yield Book* (Prentice-Hall and the New York Institute of Finance, 1972).

Thus, if we assume that all the coupons are reinvested at the same interest rate as the rate at which the bond was originally purchased, then the interest rate necessary to make the below formula valid is the YTM.

$$FV = PV \, (1 + i)^n$$

where

    FV = Future Value (or maturity value) or TDR
    PV = Present Value (or purchase price)
    $i$  = interest rate
    $n$  = number of compounding periods

**Table 2-2.** Cash Flow of a $1000, 15-Year Bond Invested at 10% and Reinvested at 8%.

| Period | SI per Period | Total Interest | Cumulative SI | Cumulative IOI |
|--------|---------------|----------------|---------------|----------------|
| 1 | $50 + ( 0.00 x 1.04) = $ 50.00 | | $ 50 | $ 0.00 |
| 2 | 50 + ( 50.00 x 1.04) = 102.00 | | 100 | 2.00 |
| 3 | 50 + ( 102.00 x 1.04) = 156.08 | | 150 | 6.08 |
| 4 | 50 + ( 156.08 x 1.04) = 212.32 | | 200 | 12.32 |
| 5 | 50 + ( 212.32 x 1.04) = 270.82 | | 250 | 20.82 |
| 6 | 50 + ( 270.82 x 1.04) = 331.65 | | 300 | 31.65 |
| 7 | 50 + ( 331.65 x 1.04) = 394.91 | | 350 | 44.91 |
| 8 | 50 + ( 394.91 x 1.04) = 460.71 | | 400 | 60.71 |
| 9 | 50 + ( 460.71 x 1.04) = 529.14 | | 450 | 79.14 |
| 10 | 50 + ( 529.14 x 1.04) = 600.31 | | 500 | 100.31 |
| 11 | 50 + ( 600.31 x 1.04) = 674.32 | | 550 | 124.32 |
| 12 | 50 + ( 674.32 x 1.04) = 751.29 | | 600 | 151.29 |
| 13 | 50 + ( 751.29 x 1.04) = 831.34 | | 650 | 180.34 |
| 14 | 50 + ( 831.34 x 1.04) = 914.60 | | 700 | 214.60 |
| 15 | 50 + ( 914.60 x 1.04) =1001.18 | | 750 | 261.18 |
| 16 | 50 + (1001.18 x 1.04) =1091.22 | | 800 | 291.22 |
| 17 | 50 + (1091.22 x 1.04) =1234.88 | | 850 | 384.88 |
| 18 | 50 + (1234.88 x 1.04) =1334.27 | | 900 | 434.27 |
| 19 | 50 + (1334.27 x 1.04) =1437.64 | | 950 | 487.64 |
| 20 | 50 + (1437.64 x 1.04) =1545.15 | | 1000 | 545.15 |
| 21 | 50 + (1545.15 x 1.04) =1659.95 | | 1050 | 609.95 |
| 22 | 50 + (1659.95 x 1.04) =1773.23 | | 1100 | 673.23 |
| 23 | 50 + (1773.23 x 1.04) =1894.16 | | 1150 | 744.16 |
| 24 | 50 + (1894.16 x 1.04) =2019.93 | | 1200 | 819.93 |
| 25 | 50 + (2019.93 x 1.04) =2150.72 | | 1250 | 900.72 |
| 26 | 50 + (2150.72 x 1.04) =2286.75 | | 1300 | 986.75 |
| 27 | 50 + (2286.75 x 1.04) =2428.22 | | 1350 | 1078.22 |
| 28 | 50 + (2428.22 x 1.04) =2575.35 | | 1400 | 1175.35 |
| 29 | 50 + (2575.35 x 1.04) =2728.37 | | 1450 | 1278.37 |
| 30 | 50 + (2728.37 x 1.04) =2887.50 | | 1500 | 1387.50 |

Table 2-3. Cash Flow for a $1,000, 15-Year Bond Reinvested at 8% with a 30% Tax Rate.

| Period | Interest Received | After-Tax Interest | Accumulated Interest & IOI | New IOI | After-Tax New IOI | Total Accumulated Interest | Cumulative After-Tax Simple Interest | Cumulative After-Tax IOI |
|---|---|---|---|---|---|---|---|---|
| 1 | $50 | $35 | $ 0.00 | $ 0.00 | $ 0.00 | $ 35.00 | $ 35 | $ 0.00 |
| 2 | 50 | 35 | 35.00 | 1.40 | 0.98 | 70.98 | 70 | 0.98 |
| 3 | 50 | 35 | 70.98 | 2.84 | 1.99 | 107.97 | 105 | 2.97 |
| 4 | 50 | 35 | 107.97 | 4.32 | 3.02 | 145.99 | 140 | 5.99 |
| 5 | 50 | 35 | 145.99 | 5.84 | 4.09 | 185.08 | 175 | 10.08 |
| 6 | 50 | 35 | 185.08 | 7.40 | 5.18 | 225.26 | 210 | 15.26 |
| 7 | 50 | 35 | 225.26 | 9.01 | 6.31 | 266.57 | 245 | 21.57 |
| 8 | 50 | 35 | 266.57 | 10.66 | 7.46 | 309.03 | 280 | 29.03 |
| 9 | 50 | 35 | 309.03 | 12.36 | 8.65 | 352.68 | 315 | 37.68 |
| 10 | 50 | 35 | 352.68 | 14.11 | 9.88 | 397.56 | 350 | 47.56 |
| 11 | 50 | 35 | 397.56 | 15.90 | 11.13 | 443.69 | 385 | 58.69 |
| 12 | 50 | 35 | 443.69 | 17.75 | 12.42 | 491.11 | 420 | 71.11 |
| 13 | 50 | 35 | 491.11 | 19.64 | 13.75 | 539.87 | 455 | 84.87 |
| 14 | 50 | 35 | 539.87 | 21.59 | 15.12 | 589.98 | 490 | 99.98 |
| 15 | 50 | 35 | 589.98 | 23.60 | 16.52 | 641.50 | 525 | 116.50 |
| 16 | 50 | 35 | 641.50 | 25.66 | 17.96 | 694.46 | 560 | 134.46 |
| 17 | 50 | 35 | 694.46 | 27.78 | 19.44 | 748.91 | 595 | 153.91 |
| 18 | 50 | 35 | 748.91 | 29.96 | 20.97 | 804.88 | 630 | 174.88 |
| 19 | 50 | 35 | 804.88 | 32.20 | 22.54 | 862.41 | 665 | 197.41 |
| 20 | 50 | 35 | 862.41 | 34.50 | 24.15 | 921.56 | 700 | 221.56 |

**Table 2-3.** (Cont.)

| Period | Interest Received | After-Tax Interest | Accumulated Interest & IOI | New IOI | After-Tax New IOI | Total Accumulated Interest | Cumulative After-Tax Simple Interest | Cumulative After-Tax IOI |
|---|---|---|---|---|---|---|---|---|
| 21 | 50 | 35 | 921.56 | 36.86 | 25.80 | 982.37 | 735 | 247.37 |
| 22 | 50 | 35 | 982.37 | 39.29 | 27.51 | 1044.87 | 770 | 274.87 |
| 23 | 50 | 35 | 1044.87 | 41.79 | 29.26 | 1109.13 | 805 | 304.13 |
| 24 | 50 | 35 | 1109.13 | 44.37 | 31.06 | 1175.18 | 840 | 335.18 |
| 25 | 50 | 35 | 1175.18 | 47.01 | 32.91 | 1243.09 | 875 | 368.09 |
| 26 | 50 | 35 | 1243.09 | 49.72 | 34.81 | 1312.90 | 910 | 402.90 |
| 27 | 50 | 35 | 1312.90 | 52.52 | 36.76 | 1384.66 | 945 | 439.66 |
| 28 | 50 | 35 | 1384.66 | 55.39 | 38.77 | 1458.43 | 980 | 478.43 |
| 29 | 50 | 35 | 1458.43 | 58.34 | 40.84 | 1534.26 | 1015 | 519.26 |
| 30 | 50 | 35 | 1534.26 | 61.37 | 42.96 | 1612.22 | 1050 | 562.22 |

***Table 2-4.*** *Net-Net-Realized Compound Yield of a $1,000, 15-Year Bond.*

| Period | Interest Received | After-Tax Tax Interest | After-Tax & Inflation Interest | Accumulated Interest & IOI | Accumulated Buying Power | New IOI | After-Tax New IOI |
|---|---|---|---|---|---|---|---|
| 1 | $50 | $35 | $15 | $ 0.00 | $ 0.00 | $ 0.00 | $ 0.00 |
| 2 | 50 | 35 | 15 | 35.00 | 15.00 | 1.40 | 0.98 |
| 3 | 50 | 35 | 15 | 70.98 | 30.42 | 2.84 | 1.99 |
| 4 | 50 | 35 | 15 | 107.97 | 46.27 | 4.32 | 3.02 |
| 5 | 50 | 35 | 15 | 145.99 | 62.57 | 5.84 | 4.09 |
| 6 | 50 | 35 | 15 | 185.08 | 79.32 | 7.40 | 5.18 |
| 7 | 50 | 35 | 15 | 225.26 | 96.54 | 9.01 | 6.31 |
| 8 | 50 | 35 | 15 | 266.57 | 114.24 | 10.66 | 7.46 |
| 9 | 50 | 35 | 15 | 309.03 | 132.44 | 12.36 | 8.65 |
| 10 | 50 | 35 | 15 | 352.68 | 151.15 | 14.11 | 9.88 |
| 11 | 50 | 35 | 15 | 397.56 | 170.38 | 15.90 | 11.13 |
| 12 | 50 | 35 | 15 | 443.69 | 190.15 | 17.75 | 12.42 |
| 13 | 50 | 35 | 15 | 491.11 | 210.48 | 19.64 | 13.75 |
| 14 | 50 | 35 | 15 | 539.87 | 231.37 | 21.59 | 15.12 |
| 15 | 50 | 35 | 15 | 589.98 | 252.85 | 23.60 | 16.52 |
| 16 | 50 | 35 | 15 | 641.50 | 274.93 | 25.66 | 17.96 |
| 17 | 50 | 35 | 15 | 694.46 | 297.63 | 27.78 | 19.44 |
| 18 | 50 | 35 | 15 | 748.91 | 320.96 | 29.96 | 20.97 |
| 19 | 50 | 35 | 15 | 804.88 | 344.95 | 32.20 | 22.54 |
| 20 | 50 | 35 | 15 | 862.41 | 369.61 | 34.50 | 24.15 |
| 21 | 50 | 35 | 15 | 921.56 | 394.96 | 36.86 | 25.80 |
| 22 | 50 | 35 | 15 | 982.37 | 421.01 | 39.29 | 27.51 |
| 23 | 50 | 35 | 15 | 1044.87 | 447.80 | 41.79 | 29.26 |
| 24 | 50 | 35 | 15 | 1109.13 | 475.34 | 44.37 | 31.06 |
| 25 | 50 | 35 | 15 | 1175.18 | 503.65 | 47.01 | 32.91 |
| 26 | 50 | 35 | 15 | 1243.09 | 532.75 | 49.72 | 34.81 |
| 27 | 50 | 35 | 15 | 1312.90 | 562.67 | 52.52 | 36.76 |
| 28 | 50 | 35 | 15 | 1384.66 | 593.42 | 55.39 | 38.77 |
| 29 | 50 | 35 | 15 | 1458.43 | 625.04 | 58.34 | 40.84 |
| 30 | 50 | 35 | 15 | 1534.26 | 657.54 | 61.37 | 42.96 |

However, if we assume that some (or all) of the coupons will be reinvested at a rate different from the bond's YTM, then the interest rate that makes the above equation correct is the RCY, and this rate will be different from the YTM.

## Net Realized Compound Yield

The *net realized compound yield* is the after-tax RCY. If the above bond was in an account that was subject to combined taxes (federal, state, city and/or personal property) of 30%, then the investor would

## Table 2-4. (Cont.)

| After-Tax & Inflation Interest | Total Accumulated Interest | Increase in Buying Power | Cumulative After-Tax Simple Interest | Cumulative After-Tax & Inflation SI | Cumulative After-Tax IOI | Cumulative After-Tax & Inflation IOI |
|---|---|---|---|---|---|---|
| $ 0.00 | $ 35.00 | 15.00 | 35 | 15 | 0.00 | 0.00 |
| 0.42 | 70.98 | 30.42 | 70 | 30 | 0.98 | 0.42 |
| 0.85 | 107.97 | 46.27 | 105 | 45 | 2.97 | 1.27 |
| 1.30 | 145.99 | 62.57 | 140 | 60 | 5.99 | 2.57 |
| 1.75 | 185.08 | 79.32 | 175 | 75 | 10.08 | 4.32 |
| 2.22 | 225.26 | 96.54 | 210 | 90 | 15.26 | 6.54 |
| 2.70 | 266.57 | 114.24 | 245 | 105 | 21.57 | 9.24 |
| 3.20 | 309.03 | 132.44 | 280 | 120 | 29.03 | 12.44 |
| 3.71 | 352.68 | 151.15 | 315 | 135 | 37.68 | 16.15 |
| 4.23 | 397.56 | 170.38 | 350 | 150 | 47.56 | 20.38 |
| 4.77 | 443.69 | 190.15 | 385 | 165 | 58.69 | 25.15 |
| 5.32 | 491.11 | 210.48 | 420 | 180 | 71.11 | 30.48 |
| 5.89 | 539.87 | 231.37 | 455 | 195 | 84.87 | 36.37 |
| 6.48 | 589.98 | 252.85 | 490 | 210 | 99.98 | 42.85 |
| 7.08 | 641.50 | 274.93 | 525 | 225 | 116.50 | 49.93 |
| 7.70 | 694.46 | 297.63 | 560 | 240 | 134.46 | 57.63 |
| 8.33 | 748.91 | 320.96 | 595 | 255 | 153.91 | 65.96 |
| 8.99 | 804.88 | 344.95 | 630 | 270 | 174.88 | 74.95 |
| 9.66 | 862.41 | 369.61 | 665 | 285 | 197.41 | 84.61 |
| 10.35 | 921.56 | 394.96 | 700 | 300 | 221.56 | 94.96 |
| 11.06 | 982.37 | 421.01 | 735 | 315 | 247.37 | 106.01 |
| 11.79 | 1044.87 | 447.80 | 770 | 330 | 274.87 | 117.80 |
| 12.54 | 1109.13 | 475.34 | 805 | 345 | 304.13 | 130.34 |
| 13.31 | 1175.18 | 503.65 | 840 | 360 | 335.18 | 143.65 |
| 14.10 | 1243.09 | 532.75 | 875 | 375 | 368.09 | 157.75 |
| 14.92 | 1312.90 | 562.67 | 910 | 390 | 402.90 | 172.67 |
| 15.75 | 1384.66 | 593.42 | 945 | 405 | 439.66 | 188.42 |
| 16.62 | 1458.43 | 625.04 | 980 | 420 | 478.43 | 205.04 |
| 17.50 | 1534.26 | 657.54 | 1015 | 435 | 519.26 | 222.54 |
| 18.41 | 1612.22 | 690.95 | 1050 | 450 | 562.22 | 240.95 |

only be able to reinvest 70% of each of the coupons received and 70% of the IOI received.

Because of the compounding effect of IOI, this decrease in the amount of money available to be reinvested has more than a 30% effect on the amount of IOI generated.

To find out how much less, let's once again construct a cash-flow chart for the above bond, assuming an 8% reinvestment rate, but let's also assume a 30% tax rate. The chart would then look like Table 2-3 (see pages 26–27).

As you can see from Table 2-3, losing 30% of each interest payment you receive to taxes reduces the TDR by 32.8%. This percentage is larger than 30% because of the cumulative effect of compounding at a 30% lower rate.

## Net-Net-Realized Compound Yield

The *net-net-realized compound yield* is the yield after the effect of both taxes and inflation are taken into account. Both of these factors serve to reduce the buying power of a given RCY. For example, if an investor in the combined (federal, state, city, personal property) 50% tax bracket was receiving 7% a year from an investment when the rate of inflation was 4%, the investor would actually be *losing* buying power.

From a $1000 investment, the above investor would receive $70 in interest per year, would have to pay $35 of that in taxes, and would be left with a $35 (3.5%) after-tax return. However, at the end of the year, the investor would need $1040 just to be able to buy what the original $1000 investment could have purchased a year earlier because of the 4% inflation. Thus, by making this investment, the investor actually loses $5 (0.5%) of purchasing power every year. The net-net-realized compound yield is most important to investors who are trying to increase their buying power.

A cash-flow chart illustrating the net-net-realized compound yield for the bond illustrated above can be found in Table 2-4 (see pages 28–29).

Thus, if an investor in the 30% tax bracket were to purchase the above bond and hold it for the full 15 years, the investor would end up with only a slight increase in buying power.

The buying power of the interest and the IOI payments is $657.54 (from Table 2-4). The buying power of the principal after 15 years of 4% inflation is $540.07 ($1000 discounted by 4%—compounded over the 15-year term).

Thus the investor would end up with a total buying power of $1197.61. Over a 15-year term, that represents a compound increase in buying power of 0.6%. Not a particularly attractive return, and not a particularly persuasive argument for investing one's money.

# CHAPTER 3

# Factors Which Affect the Degree of Uncertainty of Predicting a Given Bond's RCY

Very often a situation will arise where you want to predict a given bond's TDR and RCY. Of course, it is impossible to predict TDRs and RCYs exactly, for the reasons previously noted. However, while you cannot accurately predict what the TDR and RCY of a bond will be, you can determine the relative degree of uncertainty of one bond's TDR as compared to another.

## Principal Component

If a bond is going to be held to maturity and there are no defaults or delays in receiving the principal, then the principal component can be readily calculated by using the following formula:

$$P = \text{maturity value} + (\text{maturity value} - \text{purchase price})$$

This formula gives us exact results.

However, if the bond is going to be sold prior to its maturity, then the principal component must be estimated by estimating what the sale price of the bond is likely to be and then replacing "maturity value" in the above equation with your estimate of sale price. How accurate this formula will be is wholly dependent upon the accuracy of your estimate of the bond's future sale price.

## Interest Component

The interest component can be predicted exactly if you know the term over which you are going to own the bond. Since you know the face amount of any bond you buy and the interest rate (assuming the interest rate is fixed), you can easily calculate the interest component by using the equation:

$$\text{Interest rate} = \text{face amount} \times \text{interest rate} \times \text{term}$$

## IOI Component

On the other hand, as discussed earlier, the IOI component cannot be known in advance. It stands to reason, therefore, that any factor that increases the percentage of a bond's total return contributed by the IOI component will also increase the uncertainty of your estimate of TDR. The bigger the IOI component of a bond's total return, the larger the percentage of the bond's total return that is only "guessable."

For example, if, for bond *A*, the principal and interest components of the total return are very high, then the IOI component will be very small. A change in the reinvestment rate, and thus the IOI component, will not have a very dramatic effect on the bond's TDR. However, if, for bond *B*, the principal and interest components are very small, then even a small change in the bond's IOI will have a very dramatic effect on the bond's TDR.

As we saw in Chapter 1, the relative contribution of the IOI component in a loan is determined as follows:

1. The longer the term of the loan, the higher the IOI component will be.

2. The higher the interest rate, the higher the IOI component will be.

3. The more frequently the interest compounds, the higher the IOI component will be.

4. The higher the reinvestment rate, the higher the IOI will be.

Each of these factors also increases the IOI component of a bond. And, just as with a loan, the higher the contribution of the IOI to the TDR of a bond, the greater the uncertainty of any prediction as to the bond's TDR.

Let's examine these factors.

## Factor 1: Length of Maturity

The longer a bond has until it matures, the more time the coupons the investor receives have to compound. Thus, as the maturity lengthens, the IOI component makes up a larger and larger percentage of the total return (assuming all other factors are equal).

*Example*: The total number of dollars returned to the investor and the percentage of that total return contributed by the IOI component for the following bonds is shown in Table 3-1 (see page 34).

Bond 1: 1-year, 10% corporate bond priced at par

Bond 2: 5-year, 10% corporate bond priced at par

Bond 3: 10-year, 10% corporate bond priced at par

Bond 4: 20-year, 10% corporate bond priced at par

Bond 5: 30-year, 10% corporate bond priced at par

Thus, we can see that for the above bonds, which vary only in their maturities, the longer the maturity, the higher the percentage of the bonds' TDR contributed by the IOI. Since the IOI cannot be predicted accurately, the higher the percentage of the TDR contributed by the IOI, the greater the uncertainty of the estimate of the bond's total return.

***Table 3-1.*** *The Change in TDR and IOI for Bonds with Different Maturities.*

| No. of Bond | TDR | IOI | IOI as % of TDR |
|:---:|:---:|:---:|:---:|
| 1 | $ 1102.50 | $    2.50 | 2.27 |
| 2 | 1628.89 | 128.89 | 7.91 |
| 3 | 2653.30 | 635.30 | 23.94 |
| 4 | 7039.99 | 4039.99 | 57.39 |
| 5 | 18679.20 | 14679.20 | 78.59 |

A small percentage change in the IOI component of the short-term bond will have a negligible effect on the bond's TDR. However, even a small percentage change (10%) in the longer term bond's IOI component will have a significant effect ($1467.92) on the bond's TDR.

## Factor 2: Higher Coupon

The higher a bond's coupon, the higher the bond's cash flow. The higher the bond's cash flow, the sooner it is that more dollars are available to be reinvested. The more dollars available to be reinvested and the sooner they become available, the greater the compounding effect. The greater the compounding effect, the greater the IOI component, again assuming all other factors are equal.

*Example:* For the bonds listed below, the total return, the dollars of IOI, and the percentage of total return contributed by IOI are shown in Table 3-2 (opposite).

Bond 1: 10-year bond at par with a 4% coupon
Bond 2: 10-year bond at par with a 6% coupon
Bond 3: 10-year bond at par with an 8% coupon
Bond 4: 10-year bond at par with a 10% coupon
Bond 5: 10-year bond at par with a 12% coupon

*Table 3-2.* The Change in TDR and IOI for Bonds with Different Coupons.

| No. of Bond | TDR | IOI | IOI as % of TDR |
|:-----------:|:-----------:|:-----------:|:---------------:|
| 1 | $1485.95 | $ 85.95 | 5.78 |
| 2 | 1806.11 | 206.11 | 11.41 |
| 3 | 2191.12 | 391.12 | 17.85 |
| 4 | 2653.33 | 653.33 | 24.62 |
| 5 | 3207.14 | 1007.14 | 31.40 |

Thus we see that the percentage of the bond's TDR contributed by the IOI component increases as the coupon increases. A small percentage change in the IOI component of the low-coupon bond would have a negligible effect on the bond's TDR, but a small percentage change in the IOI component of the high-coupon bond would have a significant effect on the bond's TDR.

## Factor 3: Compounding Period

Compare the TDR for the following two bonds: A 12-year bond that pays its interest semiannually with a 12-year bond that pays its interest monthly. Both bonds are priced at par with 10% coupons.

Bond 1:
$$TDR = \$1000 \times (1 + 0.05)^{24} = \$3225.10$$
$$P = \$1000.00$$
$$I = \$1200.00$$
$$IOI = \$1025.10$$

Percentage of the TDR contributed by the IOI component:

$$\frac{\$1025.10}{\$3225.10} \times 100 = 31.79\% \text{ of TDR}$$

Bond 2:

$$TDR = \$1000 \times (1 + .01)^{144} = \$4190.62$$
$$P = \$1000.00$$
$$I = \$1200.00$$
$$IOI = \$1990.62$$

Percentage of the TDR contributed by the IOI component:

$$\frac{\$1990.62}{\$4190.62} \times 100 = 47.50\% \text{ of TDR}$$

Thus, increasing the compounding frequency increases the percentage of the TDR contributed by the IOI. Any factor that changes the bond's IOI component will have a greater impact on the TDR of a bond that compounds its interest more frequently.

### Factor 4: Reinvestment Rate

For a 10%-coupon, 5-year bond bought at par, calculate the IOI components assuming reinvestment rates of 1%, 5%, 10%, 15%, and 20% as calculated in Table 3-3 below.

As you can see, the higher the reinvestment rate, the higher the IOI component. Thus, a change in the IOI component will have a greater effect on the TDR of a bond if the reinvestment rate is high.

**Table 3-3.** *The TDR and IOI Components for Various Reinvestment Rates (10% Coupon, 5-Year Bond Bought at Par).*

| No. of Bond | Reinvestment Rate | TDR | IOI | IOI as % of TDR |
|---|---|---|---|---|
| 1 | 1% | $1511.42 | $ 11.42 | 0.76 |
| 2 | 5 | 1560.27 | 60.27 | 4.25 |
| 3 | 10 | 1628.89 | 128.89 | 7.91 |
| 4 | 15 | 1707.34 | 207.34 | 12.14 |
| 5 | 20 | 1796.94 | 296.94 | 16.52 |

## Chapter 4

# The Relationship Between Yield and Price

If, after you purchase a bond, interest rates go up, the market value of your bond will decline. This decline in market value is not permanent because, when the bond matures, it will still pay you its full face value. However, if you want to sell your bond prior to its maturity and the yields offered by similar bonds (*similar* meaning bonds offered by the same type of issuer, with the same credit rating and the same maturity) are higher, you may end up selling your bond for less than you paid for it.

Consider the following example:

On January 1, 1987, you buy a 30-year U.S. government 7% bond at par. Five years later, you wanted to sell your bond, and newly offered U.S. government 25-year bonds are yielding 12%. You will have to price your bond so that it also yields approximately 12% if you want it to be competitive in the marketplace. This means that you will have to offer your bond for about $609.95 and take a $390.05 loss. If you sell your bond for this price, your TDR for the bond over the 5-year holding period will be

***Table 4-1.*** *The Change in Market Value of a Bond Resulting from Changes in Its Yield.*

| Market Rate | Starting Bond Price | Ending Bond Price | % Change |
|---|---|---|---|
| 7% to 8% | $1000.00 | $892.59 | 10.74 |
| 8% to 9% | 892.59 | 802.38 | 10.11 |
| 9% to 10% | 802.38 | 726.16 | 9.50 |
| 10% to 11% | 726.16 | 661.37 | 8.92 |
| 11% to 12% | 661.37 | 605.95 | 8.38 |

$$\text{Principal:} \quad \$1000 + (\$1000 - \$390.05) = \$\ 609.95$$
$$\text{Interest:} \quad (\$1000 \times 0.07 \times 5) = \$\ 350.00$$
$$\text{IOI} \quad\quad\quad\quad\quad\quad = \underline{\$\ \ 60.60}$$
$$\$1020.55$$

Expressed as a percentage: To invest $1000 for five years and have a TDR of only $1020.55 means that the investor received a compound return of only 0.4% over the term of the investment. Not a very attractive return.

While understanding that the relationship between interest rates and bond prices is an *inverse* one is important, simply understanding the concept is not very useful from a practical point of view. In order to turn this concept into a useful analytical tool, you must be able to express the inverse relationship between interest rates and bond prices quantitatively.

Unfortunately, the relationship between bond prices and changing interest rates is not linear. In other words, the effect of a 1% change in the yield offered by a given bond on the bond's price depends on whether the 1% change is from 7% to 8% or from 12% to 13%.

For example, for the 30-year U.S. government bond described above, compute the percentage change in the bond's price resulting from a series of instantaneous 1% incremental increases in the bond's yield.

As the results in Table 4-1 above show, the relationship between increasing market interest rates and bond prices is not linear. Rather, the change in the market value of a bond due to a one-point rise in the bond's yield, when expresses as a percentage, *decreases* as the bond's yield increases.

Again, simply understanding this relationship is of limited practical usefulness. In order for this concept to be useful, we must be able to quantify it so that we can accurately predict how much the market value of a given bond will decline or appreciate in response to an increase or decrease in its yield resulting from an increase or decrease in market interest rates.

How do we quantify this relationship? We do so by introducing the concept of *duration*. But before we discuss duration, we need to take a step back and discuss the "time value of money" and "present-value/future-value calculations." Once we understand these concepts, we can define *duration*. We will then use duration to quantify the relationship between bond yields and bond prices.

## Present-Value/Future-Value Calculations

*A dollar paid to an investor sooner is worth more than a dollar paid later.* The reason for this is that the sooner an investor receives a dollar, the sooner it can be reinvested to earn additional interest (IOI).

Assume that you have the choice of receiving $100,000 today or $100,000 one year from today. If you receive the money today, you can immediately invest it and earn interest over the next year, whereas if you don't receive the money for a year, you cannot invest it until then. Assuming the rate of interest you can earn on $100,000 invested for one year is 10%, then you need to receive $110,000 in one year to have an offer that is equal to the $100,000 today.

Thus, given a choice between receiving $100,000 now and $115,000 a year from now, a reasonable investor with no immediate need for the funds would select the delayed payment. On the other hand, if you were faced with the choice of selecting either $100,000 now or $109,000 one year from now you would elect to receive the $100,000 now. Now let's assume that your choice is between receiving $100,000 today and X number of dollars 2 years from now (again assuming a 10% return). The number of dollars you would need to make the delayed payment equally attractive would be

Year 1: $100,000 x 1.1 = $110,000

Year 2: $110,000 x 1.1 = $121,000

Thus you would have to receive $121,000 two years from now in order to have a deal as attractive as receiving $100,000 today (assuming you can invest the funds at 10%). Expressed mathematically, the *Future Value* you need in order to equal your dollar today is:

$$FV = PV \times (1 + i)^n$$

where

FV = Future Value

PV = Present Value

i = interest rate per period (expressed as a decimal)

$n$ = number of periods

Now that we know how many dollars we need in the future to equal a dollar today, let's look at how we determine how much money we need *today* in order to have a dollar *at some point in the future*. In other words, what is the *present value* (the value today) of a dollar received at some point in the future?

To compute the present value of a future sum, we start with a dollar in the future and discount back at the assumed interest rate via the following formula:

$$PV = FV \times \frac{1}{(1 + i)^n}$$

Not surprisingly, this formula is the inverse of the one for determining the future value.

Using this formula, we determine that we would have to invest $0.78 today at 5% (compounded semiannually) in order to have a dollar 5 years from now. Thus, given our assumption about the rate, or return, we can get if we invest the money, we can conclude that $0.78 today is worth the same as a dollar 5 years from now. (That is, without taking the effect of inflation into account.)

$$PV = \$1 \times \frac{1}{(1 + 0.025)^{10}} = \$.7812$$

By the same token, a dollar today would be worth $1.28 five years from now, assuming a 5% semiannual compounded-interest rate.

$$FV = \$1 \times (1 + i)^n = \$1 \times (1 + 0.025)^{10} = \$1.28$$

Thus $.7812 today is worth a dollar five years from now and $1.28 ten years from now.

## The Present Value of a Series of Future Payments

Using the same formulas, we can determine the present value not only of one future payment but also of a series of future payments paid in succession, such as the future coupon payments a bond would pay. Take, for example, a 5-year bond bought at par that pays an investor 6% a year. The future cash flows (and the present values of those cash flows) are shown in Table 4-2 (see page 42).

One fact immediately becomes obvious from Table 4-2: When the future cash flows generated by a bond are discounted by the *bond's yield to maturity*, the sum of the present values equals the bond's purchase price. In fact, the best definition of *YTM* is: YTM is the yield which the future cash flows must be discounted by in order that the sum of the present value of the future cash flows will be equal to the bond's purchase price.

Tables 4-3 and 4-4 (see page 43) confirm this by performing the same calculations for a bond that is selling at a discount and a bond that is selling at a premium.

***Table 4-2.*** *The Present Value of a Future-Payment Stream for a Bond Purchased at Par.*

| Timing | Cash Flow | Present Value of Future Cash Flow Discounted @ 6% |
|---|---|---|
| Day 1 | − $1000 | − $1000.00 |
| 6  months | 30 | 29.13 |
| 1  year | 30 | 28.28 |
| 18  months | 30 | 27.45 |
| 2  years | 30 | 26.65 |
| 30  months | 30 | 25.88 |
| 3  years | 30 | 25.12 |
| 42  months | 30 | 24.39 |
| 4  years | 30 | 23.68 |
| 54  months | 30 | 22.99 |
| 5  years | 1030 | 766.42 |
| | $1300 | $ 00.00 |

Thus the market value of *any* security is the present value of the future cash flows discounted by a certain rate, *that rate being the YTM*.

Now that we understand the concepts of present value and future value and how they are related, let us again turn our attention to quantifying the relationship between the market price of a given security and changes in its yield.

## Quantifying the Relationship Between Yield and Price

A good starting point for this discussion is to dispel one of the great misconceptions about the relationship between interest rates and yields. Most investors who own long-term bonds groan when interest rates rise because they know the market value of their bonds will decline. While that's certainly true, it's also true that as the investor receives the bond's interest payments, those payments can be reinvested at the then higher interest rates available in the marketplace.

**Table 4-3.** *The Present Value of a Future-Payment Stream for a 5%, 5-Year Bond Priced to Offer a YTM of 7% ($916.83).*

| Timing | Cash Flow | Present Value of Future Cash Flow |
|--------|-----------|-----------------------------------|
| Day 1 | − $916.83 | − $916.83 |
| 6 months | 25.00 | 24.15 |
| 1 year | 25.00 | 23.34 |
| 18 months | 25.00 | 22.54 |
| 2 years | 25.00 | 21.78 |
| 30 months | 25.00 | 21.05 |
| 3 years | 25.00 | 20.33 |
| 42 months | 25.00 | 19.65 |
| 4 years | 25.00 | 18.98 |
| 54 months | 25.00 | 18.34 |
| 5 years | 1025.00 | 726.64 |
| | $333.17 | $000.00 |

**Table 4-4.** *The Present Value of a Future-Payment Stream for a 5%, 5-Year Bond Priced to Offer a YTM of 3% ($1092.22).*

| Timing | Cash Flow | Present Value of Future Cash Flow |
|--------|-----------|-----------------------------------|
| Day 1 | − $1092.22 | − $1092.22 |
| 6 months | 25.00 | 24.63 |
| 1 year | 25.00 | 24.27 |
| 18 months | 25.00 | 23.91 |
| 2 years | 25.00 | 23.55 |
| 30 months | 25.00 | 23.21 |
| 3 years | 25.00 | 22.86 |
| 42 months | 25.00 | 22.53 |
| 4 years | 25.00 | 22.19 |
| 54 months | 25.00 | 21.86 |
| 5 years | 1025.00 | 883.20 |
| | $157.78 | $000.00 |

Thus, when interest rates go up, bond prices decline—but this decline is *offset* by the *increase* in the amount of IOI the investor earns by reinvesting the interest payments at the then higher interest rate available in the marketplace.

Thus, when interest rates in the marketplace rise, the RCY and TDR that the investor receives is affected by two opposing factors.

### If Market Interest Rates Rise

| Lower—RCY & TDR | Higher—RCY & TDR |
|---|---|
| Loss of Market Value Resulting from Interest-Rate Risk ⟵⟶ | Increased IOI from Higher Reinvestment Rates |

Conversely, if market interest rates drop, the market value of the bond may rise, but the interest payments will be reinvested at lower and lower rates.

### If Market Interest Rates Drop

| Lower—RCY & TDR | Higher—RCY & TDR |
|---|---|
| Decreased IOI from Lower Investment Rates ⟵⟶ | Increase in Market Value Resulting from Interest-Rate Risk |

Whether the change in the amount of IOI that's earned or the change in market value exerts the greater effect on the bond's RCY depends, to a large degree, on the time horizon over which the effects are considered.

The longer the time horizon, the greater the influence that the change in IOI will have on the RCY *relative* to the influence of the change in market value.

There are two reasons for this:

First, the longer the time horizon, the greater the *change* in the IOI component (due to the effect of compounding). Thus, as time passes, the change in IOI increases its effect on the bond's TDR.

Second, any change in market value that results from a change in market interest rates will be mitigated over time as the bond's price moves toward its maturity value. Thus, as time passes, the change in market value decreases its effect on the bond's TDR.

Table 4-5 (see page 46) compares the relative effects of a decline in market value to the additional IOI earned over various time periods. As you can see from the table, as the time horizon lengthens, the change in IOI becomes more important in determining the total realized return relative to the change in market value.

The table shows the effect of a 2-point increase in market interest rates on the realized compound yield of a 30-year, 10% fixed-rate bond bought at par for various time horizons.

As you can see from Figure 4-1 (see page 47), in the early years the market decline exerts a greater effect on the market value bond than does the increase in IOI. In later years, however, the increase in IOI exerts a greater effect on the market value of the bond.

It therefore stands to reason that at some point along the bond's time horizon, the magnitudes of the increase in IOI and the decrease in market value will be equal and opposite.

The point in time where the magnitude of these two opposing forces is matched is called the bond's *duration.*

In this example, the duration of the bond is 9.46 years.

Note that while a bond's duration is a good indicator of where a given bond's reinvestment risk and interest-rate risk are matched, there is still a margin of error, and thus duration is itself an approximation and should not be relied on as an absolute.

Since this bond's duration is 9.46 years, we can expect that if an investor purchased the bond on its initial offering date and sold the bond 9 years, 5 months, and 16 days later, the investor would have a 10% RCY regardless of what happens to interest rates in the marketplace. Any market loss will be offset by an equal increase in IOI, and any gain in market value will be offset by a decrease in IOI. Unfortunately, as we shall see, the bond's "duration" also changes over time.

Table 4-5. The Effect of Interest-Rate Risk and the Increase in IOI Resulting from an Increase in Market Rates from 10% to 12% on a U.S. Government 10%, 30-Year Bond Purchased at Par.

| Years Bond Owned | Sale Price of Bond | Market Loss | Interest Paid | IOI @ 10% R-R | IOI @ 12% R-R | Extra IOI | Cumulative Effect of Market Loss & Extra IOI |
|---|---|---|---|---|---|---|---|
| 1 | $ 838.39 | $161.61 | $ 100 | $ 2.50 | $ 3.00 | $ .50 | – $ 161.31 |
| 5 | 842.38 | 157.62 | 500 | 128.89 | 159.04 | 30.15 | – 127.47 |
| 10 | 849.54 | 150.46 | 1,000 | 653.30 | 839.28 | 185.98 | 35.52 |
| 15 | 862.35 | 137.65 | 1,500 | 1,821.94 | 2,452.91 | 632.97 | 495.32 |
| 20 | 885.30 | 114.70 | 2,000 | 4,039.99 | 5,738.10 | 1,698.11 | 1,583.41 |
| 25 | 926.40 | 73.60 | 2,500 | 7,967.40 | 12,016.77 | 4,049.37 | 3,975.77 |
| 30 | 1,000.00 | 0.00 | 3,000 | 14,679.19 | 23,656.34 | 8,977.15 | 8,977.15 |

**Figure 4-1.**

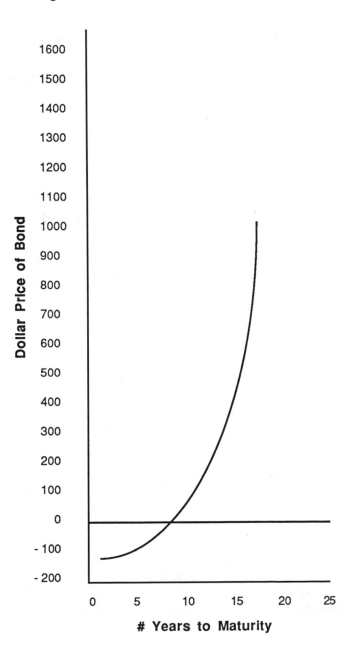

## Calculating Duration

The steps necessary to determine a given bond's duration are

1. Discount each of the cash flows the bond will pay by (the yield to maturity/# coupons per year).
2. Multiply the results of Step 1 by the number of the compounding period: 1 for the first period, 2 for the second period, and so on.
3. Add the results of Steps 1 and 2 for each period.
4. Divide the result of Step 3 by the bond's market value.
5. Divide the result of Step 4 by the number of interest payments per year.

Table 4-6 (opposite) shows the calculation for a 10-year corporate bond with a 7% coupon priced so as to offer a 10% YTM.

$$11,421.0530/1000 = 11.4211$$

Divide 11.4210530 by the number of interest payments per year.

$$11.4210530/2 = 5.712$$

Thus

This bond's duration = 5.712.

## Uses of Duration

Calculating a bond's duration is not just an intellectual exercise. You can use this information in several ways.

First, you can use it to increase the return of your bond portfolio over a given time horizon. For example, let's assume you want to

*Table 4-6.* The Duration Calculation of a 10-Year, 7% Coupon Bond Priced to Offer a 10% YTM.

| Period | Cash Flow | PV of CF | PV x CF | PV x CF x Period |
|--------|-----------|----------|---------|------------------|
| 1 | $ 35 | 0.9524 | $ 33.33 | 33.3340 |
| 2 | 35 | 0.9070 | 31.75 | 63.4921 |
| 3 | 35 | 0.8638 | 30.23 | 90.7029 |
| 4 | 35 | 0.8227 | 28.79 | 115.1783 |
| 5 | 35 | 0.7835 | 27.42 | 137.1171 |
| 6 | 35 | 0.7462 | 26.12 | 156.7052 |
| 7 | 35 | 0.7107 | 24.87 | 174.1169 |
| 8 | 35 | 0.6768 | 23.69 | 189.5150 |
| 9 | 35 | 0.6446 | 22.56 | 203.0518 |
| 10 | 35 | 0.6139 | 21.49 | 214.8696 |
| 11 | 35 | 0.5847 | 20.46 | 225.1015 |
| 12 | 35 | 0.5568 | 19.49 | 233.8717 |
| 13 | 35 | 0.5303 | 18.56 | 241.2962 |
| 14 | 35 | 0.5051 | 17.68 | 247.4833 |
| 15 | 35 | 0.4810 | 16.84 | 252.5250 |
| 16 | 35 | 0.4581 | 16.03 | 256.5425 |
| 17 | 35 | 0.4363 | 15.27 | 259.5965 |
| 18 | 35 | 0.4155 | 14.54 | 261.7780 |
| 19 | 35 | 0.3957 | 13.85 | 263.1631 |
| 20 | 1,035 | 0.3769 | 390.08 | 7801.6123 |
|  |  |  |  | 11,421.0530 |

make an investment, but you will need your money back in 10 years. In other words, your *investment horizon* is 10 years. With this constraint, you have the choice of either buying a bond that matures in 10 years or buying a bond whose duration is 10 years.

With the first option, you know that you will receive the return of your principal plus whatever the bond pays in interest payments plus whatever IOI you earn by reinvesting the coupons in progressively shorter-term bonds that all matured on or about the same date. Thus your first coupon would be invested in a vehicle maturing in 9½ years, your second coupon in a vehicle that matures in 9 years, and so on.

However, with the second option, you know that when you sell your bond, any market *loss* will be approximately offset by an increase in the IOI you have earned and any market *gain* will be approximately offset by a reduction in the IOI. The advantage of using the second option is that it allows you to buy a bond with a longer term (and thus, usually, a higher yield) than a 10-year bond.

You can do the same thing with the coupon payments. Rather than reinvesting the first coupon in a bond with a 9¹/₂-year *maturity,* you can reinvest it in a bond with a 9¹/₂-year *duration* and again earn a higher return.

Thus, by allowing you to determine the time frame at which the interest-rate risk and the reinvestment risk for a given are approximately balanced, duration allows you to buy a bond whose maturity, coupon, and YTM are such that *the bond itself is a self-contained hedge against interest-rate and reinvestment risk for a time period of your choosing.*

## Quantifying Bond Volatility

Earlier in this chapter, we mentioned that duration provides a way to quantify the relationship between a given bond's market value and its yield. Duration does have a reasonably accurate linear relationship with changes in market value due to changes in market interest rate after it is modified by dividing it as follows:

$$\frac{\text{Duration}}{1 + (\text{YTM}/2)}$$

(YTM expressed as a decimal)

The result of this calculation is called the *modified duration.*

Thus, the modified duration of a corporate bond with a duration of 7 years and a YTM of 10% would be

$$\text{Modified duration} = \frac{7}{1 + (0.1/2)} = \frac{7}{1.05} = 6.67$$

The formula for percentage change in a bond's price is

$$\% \text{ change in bp} = - (\text{modified duration}) \times \frac{\text{Change in market yield in basis points}}{100}$$

Thus, if the market yield for comparable bonds with comparable credit ratings and maturities increases by 2 percentage points (200 basis points), the percentage change in the market price of the bond will be approximately:

$$\% \text{ change} = - 6.67 \times 200/100 = -13.34\% \text{ in market value}$$

Thus the percentage change in a bond's price in response to a change in market rates *is approximately a linear function of duration after the duration is modified.*

### Factors Which Affect Volatility

A bond's *volatility* can be defined as a measure of the magnitude of a given bond's change in market value in response to an instantaneous change in market interest rates. This definition includes the word *instantaneous* to separate the change in market value due to a sudden change in interest rates from the change in market value that a bond selling at a discount or premium experiences as it approaches its maturity date (due to the amortization of a discount or a premium).

The three principal factors which affect a given bond's volatility are

1. the bond's coupon
2. the bond's maturity
3. the bond's initial yield.

The higher the bond's coupon, the lower the bond's volatility. The reason for this is that the higher the coupon, the higher the cash flow paid to the bondholder. The more cash flow the investor receives, the more dollars available to be reinvested at the then current rate (be it higher or lower). Since there are more dollars available to be invested at the then current rate, the market value of the first bond does not have to change as much in order for it to be as attractive as a bond with a lower coupon.

Consider the case of two 20-year bonds—each priced so as to offer a 7% YTM and identical in every way except for the size of their coupons. We'll assume that the first bond has a coupon of 7% (thus its market value is $1000) and the second bond has a coupon of 3% (thus its market value is $572.90).

If market yields for similar bonds suddenly rise to 10%, the first bond will drop in market value to $742.61 while the second bond will drop in value to $399.43. Thus the first bond will experience only a 25.75% decline in value while the second bond experiences a 30.28% decline in market value. Thus the first bond is significantly less volatile than the second bond.

The reason for this is that the first bond pays its investor $70 a year in interest while the second bond pays its investor only $30 a year. This means that the first investor has an additional $40 per year that can be reinvested at the higher rate of 10%. During the second year, the first investor receives another $40 that can be reinvested at 10% *plus* the IOI (at 10%) that the first additional $40 would have earned.

Thus, over time, the advantage of the first bond over the second bond compounds, resulting in an even greater advantage for the first bond. This is why two bonds with the same initial YTM but different coupons experience such different changes in price in response to changing market interest rates.

This interaction between the bond's price, coupon, and reinvestment rate works to the *disadvantage* of the investor who purchases the first bond if market interest rates decline. If market rates decline, the first investor has more dollars being reinvested faster at the then lower market interest rate, and thus the price of the first bond will not have to change as much as the price of the second bond in order for both bonds to have the same YTM. Thus the first bond will not experience as much price appreciation.

From a strategic point of view, investors should buy high-coupon bonds when they expect interest rates to rise and low-coupon (or zero-coupon) bonds when they expect interest rates to fall.

The second factor, the bond's maturity, affects volatility because the longer a bond's term, the more time there is for the interest to compound at the new market interest rate and thus the greater the effect that the new market interest rate will have on the bond's TDR and RCY. *Thus for a given bond (all other factors being equal) the longer the term, the greater the bond's volatility.*

From a strategic point of view, investors should buy short-term bonds (or bonds with short durations) when interest rates are expected to rise and long-term bonds (or bonds with long durations) when interest rates are expected to fall.

The last factor, the initial yield, affects the volatility of a given bond because, for a given percentage change in the bond's yield, the higher the initial yield, the greater the change in yield is, when the yield is expressed in basis points. This sounds more complicated than it is. For example, consider a 4% bond at par. If market rates go up 25%, the rate for new bonds would be 5% (a 100-basis-point difference). However, if the initial rate was 10% and rates go up 25%, the new rate will be 12.5%, or a 250-basis-point increase in yield. Thus, for a given percentage increase in yield, the higher the initial yield, the greater the change in yield (expressed in basis points).

Thus, the higher the initial yield, the more prices are going to change as a result of a percentage increase in market yields.

# Chapter 5

# Settlement and Accrued Interest

Up until now we have examined bond yields but have not taken accrued interest into account. This was done for the sake of simplicity, but we will now consider accrued interest and its effect on a bond's yield(s). However, before we can discuss accrued interest we will have to discuss settlement.

## Settlement

When a buyer and seller agree to enter into a bond transaction, they do so on what is called the *trade date*. On this date, they agree to the sale price and delivery terms. The buyer and seller actually exchange cash and securities on a specified date after the trade date; this date is called the *settlement date*.

For most types of bonds (corporates, municipals, most agencies), this date is five *business* days after the trade date. Legal holidays and weekends are not included in these five days. U.S. government bonds settle one business day after the trade date. So, if we were to buy a corporate bond and a government bond on July 3, then the settlement dates for these trades would be July 11 for the corporate bond and July 7 for the government bond, assuming the following calendar:

| JULY | | | | | | |
|---|---|---|---|---|---|---|
| S | M | T | W | T | F | S |
| | | 1 | 2 | 3 | 4 | 5 |
| 6 | 7 | 8 | 9 | 10 | 11 | 12 |
| 13 | 14 | 15 | 16 | 17 | 18 | 19 |
| 20 | 21 | 22 | 23 | 24 | 25 | 26 |
| 27 | 28 | 29 | 30 | 31 | | |

### Accrued Interest

*Accrued interest* is the interest that the seller is entitled to receive from the buyer on settlement date. Accrued interest represents the interest that the seller has earned by owning the bond for a time period after the last interest-payment date. Perhaps the best way to understand accrued interest is to review some examples, starting with a corporate-bond example.

*Example 1:* Let's assume a corporate bond pays its interest to owners of record on February 1 and August 1, and let's assume the following calendar:

| FEBRUARY | | | | | | |
|---|---|---|---|---|---|---|
| S | M | T | W | T | F | S |
| | 1 | 2 | 3 | 4 | 5 | 6 |
| 7 | 8 | 9 | 10 | 11 | 12 | 13 |
| 14 | 15 | 16 | 17 | 18 | 19 | 20 |
| 21 | 22 | 23 | 24 | 25 | 26 | 27 |
| 28 | | | | | | |

| MARCH |     |     |     |     |     |     |
| --- | --- | --- | --- | --- | --- | --- |
| S   | M   | T   | W   | T   | F   | S   |
|     | 1   | 2   | 3   | 4   | 5   | 6   |
| 7   | 8   | 9   | 10  | 11  | 12  | 13  |
| 14  | 15  | 16  | 17  | 18  | 19  | 20  |
| 21  | 22  | 23  | 24  | 25  | 26  | 27  |
| 28  | 29  | 30  | 31  |     |     |     |

| APRIL |     |     |     |     |     |     |
| --- | --- | --- | --- | --- | --- | --- |
| S   | M   | T   | W   | T   | F   | S   |
|     |     |     |     | 1   | 2   | 3   |
| 4   | 5   | 6   | 7   | 8   | 9   | 10  |
| 11  | 12  | 13  | 14  | 15  | 16  | 17  |
| 18  | 19  | 20  | 21  | 22  | 23  | 24  |
| 25  | 26  | 27  | 28  | 29  | 30  |     |

If a trade is entered into on April 6, it will settle on April 13. The number of days from the last interest-payment date to the settlement date will be 72. Why 72? Well, for the purpose of calculating the accrued interest on a *corporate bond*, every month is assumed to have 30 days and each year to have 360 days. Thus, the month of February is assumed to have 30 days even though it really has 28 days, and the month of March is assumed to have 30 days even though it really has 31 days. For the month of April, the number of days is equal to the actual number of days to *the day prior to the* settlement date, April 12 in this example.

Therefore, the total number of days is equal to:

| February | 30 days |
| --- | --- |
| March | 30 days |
| April | 12 days |
|  | 72 days |

Once we know the number of days between the last interest-payment date and the settlement date, we can calculate the accrued interest. The formula is

Accrued interest = principal x rate x time

For a corporate, municipal, and most agency bonds:

Principal = face amount of the trade

Rate = coupon rate (expressed as a %)

Time = number of days as calculated above/360 (12 x 30)

If we bought $10,000 (face amount) worth of bonds that had a 9% coupon, accrued interest would be

$$\$10{,}000 \times 0.09 \times (72/360) = \$180$$

We would therefore have to pay the seller $180 to compensate the seller for owning the bond from February 1 until settlement date.

*Example 2:* If, instead of the above bond, we purchased a corporate bond on April 20 that had an 8% coupon and paid its interest on February 15 and August 15, the settlement date would be April 27, and the number of days for which interest was due would be calculated as follows:

February 15–March 15 = 30 days
March 15–April 15 = 30 days
April 15–April 26 = <u>11 days</u>
71 days

Using the formula for accrued interest, we would arrive at the following:

$$\$10{,}000 \times 0.08 \times (71/360) = \$157.77$$

*Example 3:* If the bonds in the above two examples were U.S. government bonds, we would have to make two adjustments to our formula.

1. The settlement dates, and thus the number of days from the last interest payment to the day before settlement, would be different.

2. We would not make the assumption that there were 30 days per month and 360 days per year. Instead, we would use the actual number of days in each month and the actual number of days in the year in the "time" component.

So if we substitute a government bond for the corporate bond in Example 1, the settlement date would be April 8, and the number of days until settlement would be calculated as follows:

| | |
|---|---|
| February | 28 days |
| March | 31 days |
| April | 7 days |
| | 66 days |

Thus the calculation would become

$$\$10,000 \times 0.09 \times (66/365) = \$163.19$$

*Example 4:* If we substitute a government bond for the corporate bond in Example 2, the settlement date would be April 21 and the number of days to settlement would be calculated as follows:

| | |
|---|---|
| February | 13 days |
| March | 31 days |
| April | 20 days |
| | 64 days |

Thus the calculation would become

$$\$10,000 \times (64/365) = \$140.27$$

## *The Effect of Accrued Interest on Yield*

Let's consider what happens when we buy a bond in between its two coupon payment dates and pay the seller the accrued interest to which he or she is entitled.

For the sake of simplicity, let's assume we buy a corporate bond with a 12% coupon right in the middle of two coupon dates for par. Because the bond is a corporate bond and has a 12% coupon, the interest accrued each month is an even $10.

Because we bought the bond in the middle of two coupon dates, we owe the seller $30 in accrued interest for the three months that the seller owned the bond after the last interest-payment date. Thus, the total purchase price of the bond is $1030 ($1000 purchase price plus $30 accrued interest.)

Three months after purchasing the bond, we receive $60, the full coupon payment, even though we only owned the bond for three months and are only entitled to three months' worth of interest. In effect, then, we are "reimbursed" for the accrued interest we paid to the seller. Of course we are reimbursed three months *after* we paid the accrued interest to the seller. This means that for those three months, we do not have the use of our $30. It is $30 that we cannot invest until three months later. Our loss, therefore, is the interest our $30 *could have earned* over those three months.

If we assume that the $30 could have been invested at a 6% annual rate over three months, that $30 could have earned us 1.5%, or $0.45. If another investor had been able to buy another bond with the same coupon and price but on its interest-payment date instead of between interest-payment dates, that investor would not have had to tie up $30 for three months and so would be $0.45 ahead of us.

While $0.45 may not sound like a big deal, consider the effect accrued interest could have on a portfolio's TDR if we were purchasing $50,000,000 worth of the bonds. The accrued interest would then be $1,500,000, and the lost interest on this sum would be $22,500. Thus the effect of accrued interest on yield is no small concern for anyone managing a sizable portfolio.

## Chapter 6

# Effect of Calls and Puts On Yield

## Call Provisions

If a bond is *callable*, the issuer has the option of forcing the redemption of the bond prior to its stated maturity date. Many corporate bonds are callable at some point during their term; however, a bond is usually not callable for the first five or ten years after it is issued. During this time, the bond is said to have *call protection*.

After the period of call protection has passed, the bond may become callable either at any time or only on certain dates (usually dates that are anniversaries of the bond's issue date), depending upon the terms outlined in the bond's indenture.

Generally, when a bond is called as soon as it becomes callable, the issuer pays the bondholder a small premium over par to compensate the investor for the inconvenience of losing the bond. As time passes, however, most callable bonds generally become callable at progressively lower prices until, finally, they are callable at par.

For example, let's assume that XYZ Corporation issues $50,000,000 worth of a 12%, 15-year bond. However, XYZ's CFO believes that interest rates will decline over the next few years and so wants to have the option of refinancing these bonds with new, lower-yielding bonds five years from now.

To have this option, the CFO includes a call provision in the original bond indenture that gives XYZ Corporation the option of calling the bonds at the following times and prices:

On the 5-year anniversary of the bond's issue date at a price of 103
On the 7-year anniversary at a price of 102
On the 9-year anniversary at a price of 101
On the 10-year anniversary or any anniversary thereafter at par

If, five years from the date the bonds were originally issued, interest rates are, indeed, substantially lower (let's assume they are 7%), the company will call its original bonds and issue a new series of 10-year bonds yielding 7%. Thus, rather than paying interest over the next ten years, the company reduces its cost of borrowing to 7%, a 5% annual savings in its interest expense.

Of course if, at the 5-year anniversary date, interest rates are equal to or higher than 12%, XYZ will probably not exercise its call option, and the bonds will continue to stay in existence unless, of course, XYZ no longer needs to borrow money, in which case it will call the bonds regardless of current interest rates.

Because the bonds in this example are not callable for the first five years, they are said to offer *5-year call protection*. Also, if the bonds in this example are not called on the 5-year anniversary, then the bonds have another two years of call protection until the 7-year anniversary.

Call provisions vary widely from issue to issue, so it's important to review the specific call provisions of any bond you consider buying or selling. Some bonds have call provisions that require the issuer to call the entire issue; other issues are subject to partial calls. A *partial call* occurs when the company only forces the redemption of *part* of its outstanding bond issue. The bonds selected for redemption in a partial call are usually selected at random.

From an investor's point of view, a call option is almost always negative. Most companies call their debt only when the interest rate the company's bonds are paying is higher than the current interest rate (except in the case of "sinking fund bonds," discussed in the next chapter). In other words, an investor who buys a bond that is callable risks losing the bond if the yield that the bond offers is relatively attractive to the market interest rates on a call date.

A call option has another detrimental effect on a bond investment: It limits the upside potential of a bond's market value. The reason for this is that any potential buyer must take into account the fact that the bond might be called prior to its maturity date. Thus any buyer will compute the yield to the call date as well as the yield to the maturity date before bidding for the bond.

Consider the following:

A corporate bond with a 10% coupon is callable in 5 years and matures in 30 years. If current interest rates in the marketplace for comparable 5-year paper is 7% and for comparable 30-year paper is 8%, what is this bond worth?

Well, if you price the bond so as to yield 8% over 30 years (i.e., as if it were *noncallable*), the bond will be worth $1226.23.

But, if you price the bond so as to yield 7% over five years, then it is only worth $1124.75. The difference between the two valuations is thus $101.48. In this case, the call option serves to limit the upside potential of the bond severely by requiring that any premium over the par be amortized over a shorter time period. In this example, rather than a $226.23 premium being amortized over 30 years ($7.54 per year), a $124.75 premium is amortized over 5 years ($24.95 per year).

## Discount Bonds and Call Provisions

Just because a bond is selling at a discount to its par value on the day you purchase it does not mean that you can ignore the bond's call provisions. If, several years after you purchase the bond, interest rates drop, the call provisions you ignored may come back to haunt you.

*Example 1:* Let's assume that you buy a 30-year corporate bond with a 9% coupon that's priced to yield 10% (i.e., the market value of the bond is $905.35). Since the bond is selling at a discount, you ignore the call provisions, which include annual call options at par starting in five years. Three years later, however, long-term market interest rates drop to a point where long-term bonds with comparable maturities are yielding 7%. Your bond, if it were noncallable, would be worth $1241.13 if it were priced to yield 7% over 27 years. However, since your bond is callable in another two years, it has to be priced like 2-year paper. Thus, your bond will probably have a market value of only about $1036.73 (priced to yield 7% over 2 years).

Thus, to properly analyze a bond that's callable, you have to include an analysis of the effect that the bond's call provisions will have on both the bond's *term* and on the bond's *price* in *light of your expectations about interest rates.* Buying long-term bonds because you expect interest rates to drop is futile if the bonds you select are callable.

A better alternative might be to buy another bond that had a slightly lower yield that was noncallable.

*Example 2:* Let's assume that you buy a 30-year corporate bond with an 8³/4% coupon that's priced to yield 9¹/2%. Initially, the bond will yield less than the bond in Example 1, but if interest rates drop, the bond's market value will rise to $1210.99 (priced to yield 7% over 27 years) and thus will be a much better investment.

If interest rates stay flat, the bond in Example 1 will be a better investment. Thus the selection of which bond to buy really depends on what your projections for future interest rates are and how accurate your projections are.

You also need to consider how the bond's call provisions will affect the bond's duration, TDR, and RCY. A bond that's callable will have different durations, RCYs, and TDRs, depending upon whether or not it is called. Thus callable bonds are often unsuitable if your objective is to fund a specific future liability.

## Put Provisions

The opposite of a call provision is a put provision. A *put provision* is a right granted to the investor by the issuer that gives the investor the option of forcing the issuer to repurchase the bond at a certain price (almost always par) on a certain date or dates prior to the bond's stated maturity date. Thus the investor who owns a bond with a put provision has the option of shortening the maturity of the bond to the bond's put date(s). The investor would elect to exercise this right if market interest rates rose after the investor purchased the bond. If interest rates are higher on the put date, the investor can put his bond back to the issuer, get his capital back, and reinvest it at the then higher rate available in the marketplace.

For example, suppose an investor purchases a 10-year corporate bond at par yielding 8%. If, two years later, market rates for 8-year bonds are 10%, the value of the investor's bond will be $891.62 (8%, 8-year bond priced to yield 10%). If the bond were putable at the 2-year mark at par, the investor would be able to put the bond back to the issuer at par and then reinvest his entire $1000 in another bond yielding 10%. Thus, by having the put option, the investor would be able to increase his capital by $108.38 *and* increase his current return from 8% to 10%.

This is not as good as it sounds, however, because bonds with put provisions usually offer yields that are substantially lower than yields on nonputable paper, i.e., the investor has to *buy* the put provision by accepting a lower yield. Of course, putable bonds also offer yields that are slightly higher than bonds with a final maturity date equal to the put date. Thus, if 2-year bonds yield 6%, and 10-year bonds yield 9%, then 10-year bonds with put provisions every two years might yield 6 1/2%.

Whether or not putable bonds are the best investment depends on what happens to interest rates. If interest rates go up substantially, then having the option of reclaiming your principal may be worth more than the 2 1/2% yield advantage that the 10-year nonputable bond offers. However, if interest rates go up only slightly, or decline, then the straight 10-year bond is the better buy.

Thus choosing which bond is more attractive depends on:

1. your expectations of future interest rates
2. the accuracy of those expectations
3. your tolerance for risk if your expectations are wrong.

# Chapter 7

# Sinking-Fund Bonds

Many municipal and corporate bond issues have sinking-fund provisions. A *sinking fund* is a fund that the issuer creates for the purpose of periodically buying back and retiring part of an outstanding bond issue in accordance with the terms and conditions outlined in the bond's indenture.

## Why Have a Sinking Fund?

The principal reason for establishing a sinking fund is to make the bond more attractive to potential investors. For example, let's assume a company issues $1,000,000 worth of a 10%, 20-year bond. If the bonds are neither called nor put during their term, then in 20 years the issuer will have a liability to the investors of $105,000,000 (the principal due the investor plus the last interest payment).

Investors, however, may be uncomfortable with the company's ability (or willingness!) to periodically set aside enough cash to meet a future liability of this size.

**Table 7-1.** *The Outstanding Balance and the Interest Expense of a Sinking-Fund Bond.*

| Year | Amount of Bonds Outstanding* | Annual Interest Expense* | Annual Dollar Outlay* |
|------|------------------------------|--------------------------|-----------------------|
| 1    | 100                          | 10.00                    | 10.00                 |
| 2    | 100                          | 10.00                    | 10.00                 |
| 3    | 100                          | 10.00                    | 10.00                 |
| 4    | 100                          | 10.00                    | 10.00                 |
| 5    | 100                          | 10.00                    | 10.00                 |
| 6    | 100                          | 10.00                    | 10.00                 |
| 7    | 100                          | 10.00                    | 10.00                 |
| 8    | 100                          | 10.00                    | 10.00                 |
| 9    | 100                          | 10.00                    | 10.00                 |
| 10   | 100                          | 10.00                    | 10.00                 |
| 11   | 95                           | 9.50                     | 14.75                 |
| 12   | 90                           | 9.00                     | 14.50                 |
| 13   | 85                           | 8.50                     | 14.25                 |
| 14   | 80                           | 8.00                     | 14.00                 |
| 15   | 75                           | 7.50                     | 13.75                 |
| 16   | 70                           | 7.00                     | 13.50                 |
| 17   | 65                           | 6.50                     | 13.25                 |
| 18   | 60                           | 6.00                     | 13.00                 |
| 19   | 55                           | 5.50                     | 12.75                 |
| 20   | 50                           | 5.00                     | 55.00                 |

*All figures in millions

One way to solve this problem is for the company to agree to retire small portions of the bond issue periodically prior to its stated maturity date instead of trying to retire the entire issue at once. For example, let's assume the company includes a sinking-fund provision in its bond indenture that requires it to retire $5,000,000 (face amount) worth of bonds every year for each of the last 10 years the issue is outstanding.

Under this provision, the amount of debt that the company will have outstanding at the end of each year and the company's annual interest expense for each year will be as shown in Table 7-1 above.

Thus, by establishing a sinking fund and using the money in that fund to retire a portion of the bond issue periodically, the company reduces its final payment in 20 years from $105,000,000 to $52,500,000, a level that may be more palatable to the potential investor.

## Redeeming Bonds Selling at a Discount

When the company retires a portion of a bond issue, it usually does so at the same time each year throughout the period that the sinking fund is in effect. If the bonds are selling in the open market at a discount to their face value, the company (or more likely its agent) will try to buy the proscribed amount of the bonds in the open market. For example, if at the first sinking-fund date, the bonds are selling in the open market for a price of 90, then repurchasing $5,000,000 (face amount) of the bonds will cost the issuing company $4,500,000.

Usually, however, Wall Street does not make it that easy for an issuing company to repurchase its bonds. If, in this example, the company starts repurchasing its bonds approximately every January 15 (in accordance with the provisions in its indenture), then, beginning around November, shrewd investors will start buying and hoarding the company's bonds. If, in January, the company cannot buy enough bonds at 90 to meet its sinking-fund requirements, then it will have to bid progressively higher prices until it attracts enough bonds.

Since the company *has to buy* $5,000,000 (face amount) of the bonds every January the sinking fund is in effect, the company is at a severe disadvantage in the marketplace. If investors have squirreled away enough of the company's bonds, the company may not be able to find $5,000,000 worth of the bonds available at 90 (the bond's fair-market value). If this happens, the company will have to offer a succession of higher bids (in effect *overpaying* to repurchase its own bonds) until it is able to attract enough bonds to meet its sinking-fund requirement.

If we assume that the company is able to purchase the $5,000,000 worth at the prices shown in Table 7-2 (see page 70), then the company will end up paying $100,000 more than it theoretically should have in order to meet its sinking-fund requirement. That extra

**Table 7-2.** The Cost of Meeting a Sinking-Fund Requirement.

| Dollar Amount | Price | Premium over True Value |
|---|---|---|
| $1,000,000 | $900 | $      0 |
| 1,000,000 | 910 | 10,000 |
| 1,000,000 | 920 | 20,000 |
| 1,000,000 | 930 | 30,000 |
| 1,000,000 | 940 | 40,000 |
| | | $100,000 |

$100,000 goes to the shrewd investors who hoarded the company's *bonds* and then resold the bonds to the company (at a profit!).

If one of our shrewd investors becomes overly greedy and holds out for a bid of more than $940 per bond, the investor will not sell his bonds to the company and will either be stuck holding the bonds for another year or will have to sell them (probably at a loss). Thus, investors who play the sinking-fund game compete against each other as well as against the issuing company.

## Redeeming Bonds Selling at a Premium

If the bonds are selling at a premium to their face value, the company (which is usually prevented from paying more than par in order to meet a sinking-fund requirement) will not be able to buy any bonds on the open market. Instead, it will have to resort to calling the bonds (as discussed in the last chapter) in order to meet its sinking-fund requirements.

Unlike a regular call, however, the issuer will not call all of the outstanding bonds but, instead, will call only enough bonds to meet the sinking-fund requirement (i.e., a partial call).

## Mathematics of Sinking-Fund-Bonds' Yields

Let's assume the bond above is selling at a price of 110 and the investor buys 100 bonds for a current yield of 9.09% (10/110) at the *start* of the ninth year in which the bond is in existence. Since no bonds have been called, put, or redeemed at this point , the company will still have the entire issue ($100,000,000 worth) outstanding.

At the start of year 10, however, the company has to retire $5,000,000 worth of the issue. Since the bonds are selling at a premium, the company will have to call the bonds in order to meet its sinking-fund requirement.

If this call (like most calls) is a random call, then, statistically, 1 out of every 20 bonds outstanding will be called. If you own 100 bonds, you will probably lose 5 bonds to the call. *Note*, however, that since the bonds that are selected to be called are selected randomly, if you own 100 of the bonds, you may actually have more or less than 5 of your bonds called. The actual number of bonds you have called is a very significant factor in determining your yield. The larger the number of bonds you own, the closer the actual number of bonds that are called away from you is likely to be to the statistical expectation.

If we assume that you purchased 100 of the bonds at the beginning of the ninth year, then you would earn $10,000 in interest over the ninth year and, assuming an 8% reinvestment rate, $200 in IOI.

In the beginning of year 10, however, you would have 5 bonds (statistically) called at par. So, over year 10, your cash flows would be

| | |
|---|---|
| Start of year 10—lose 5 bonds at par | + $5,000.00 |
| Loss of principal (5 bonds at $100 per bond) | – $  500.00 |
| Middle-of-year-10 interest payment | + $4,750.00 |
| End-of-year-10 interest payment | + $4,750.00 |
| IOI on year-9's interest ($10,200 at 8%) | + $  832.32 |
| IOI on year-10's interest ($4,750 at 8%) | + $  190.00 |
| IOI on return of principal ($5,000 at 8%) | + $  408.00 |

Thus, an investor who purchased 100 bonds in year 9 for $110,000 would (statistically) have a return of $25,630.32 and would be left with 95 bonds at the start of the following year.

The next year, the investor again would lose 5 bonds to the call (statistically), but the percentage of the investor's bonds that would

*Table 7-3.* Percentage of Bonds Called Per Year.

| Year Sinking Fund Is in Effect | Number of Bonds Owned | Number of Bonds Called | Percentage of Bonds Called |
|---|---|---|---|
| 1 | 100 | 5 | 5.00 |
| 2 | 95 | 5 | 5.26 |
| 3 | 90 | 5 | 5.56 |
| 4 | 85 | 5 | 5.88 |
| 5 | 80 | 5 | 6.25 |
| 6 | 75 | 5 | 6.67 |
| 7 | 70 | 5 | 7.14 |
| 8 | 65 | 5 | 7.69 |
| 9 | 60 | 5 | 8.33 |
| 10 | 55 | 5 | 9.09 |

be lost is higher because the investor had only 95 bonds at the beginning of the year. Thus, over time, the percentage of bonds that are lost increases (see Table 7-3 above).

Now it's impossible to call part of a bond (such as 0.26 in year 2), but in years 1 and 2, the probability is that the investor will lose 5 bonds; in years 4 and 5, the probability is that the investor will lose 6 bonds, and so on.

## The TDR Return of Sinking-Fund Bonds

As always:

$$TDR = P + I + IOI$$

The number of dollars of *principal* is simply equal to the number of bonds multiplied by their maturity value. In this example:

$$100 \times \$1000 = \$100,000$$

The number of dollars of *interest* is equal to the *sum* of the (coupon x principal x number of years) for each period for which there is a dif-

**Table 7-4.** *The Tabulation of Interest for a Sinking-Fund Bond.*

| *(Coupon x Principal x No. of Years)* |
|---|
| (.1) x ($100,000) x (10) = $100,000 |
| (.1) x ($ 95,000) x (1) = $ 9,500 |
| (.1) x ($ 90,000) x (1) = $ 9,000 |
| (.1) x ($ 85,000) x (1) = $ 8,500 |
| (.1) x ($ 80,000) x (1) = $ 8,000 |
| (.1) x ($ 75,000) x (1) = $ 7,500 |
| (.1) x ($ 70,000) x (1) = $ 7,000 |
| (.1) x ($ 65,000) x (1) = $ 6,500 |
| (.1) x ($ 60,000) x (1) = $ 6,000 |
| (.1) x ($ 55,000) x (1) = $ 5,500 |
| (.1) x ($ 50,000) x (1) = $ 5,000 |
| $172,500 |

ferent number of the original bonds outstanding. The tabulation of interest for a sinking-fund bond is shown in Table 7-4 above.

## IOI Component

The *IOI* component is equal to the interest plus the principal *received during each period* multiplied by $(1 + i)^n$ where $i$ is the assumed reinvestment rate per period and $n$ is the number of periods the money received can compound. Table 7-5 (see page 74) illustrates the IOI component of a sinking-fund bond.

$$\$515,392.31 - \$172,500 \text{ (int.)} - \$50,000 \text{ (principal)}$$
$$= (IOI = \$287,892)$$

The three components of this bond's TDR therefore are

$$\text{TDR} = P + I + IOI$$
$$= \$100,000 + \$172,500 + \$287,892$$
$$= \$560,392$$

**Table 7-5.** The IOI Component of a Sinking-Fund Bond.

| End of Period | Interest Received at End of Period | Principal Received at End of Period | Number of Compounding Periods @ 4% | TDR for Period |
|---|---|---|---|---|
| 1 | $5,000 | 0 | 39 | $ 23,081.83 |
| 2 | 5,000 | 0 | 38 | 22,194.07 |
| 3 | 5,000 | 0 | 37 | 21,340.45 |
| 4 | 5,000 | 0 | 36 | 20,519.66 |
| 5 | 5,000 | 0 | 35 | 19,730.45 |
| 6 | 5,000 | 0 | 34 | 18,971.58 |
| 7 | 5,000 | 0 | 33 | 18,241.91 |
| 8 | 5,000 | 0 | 32 | 17,540.29 |
| 9 | 5,000 | 0 | 31 | 16,865.67 |
| 10 | 5,000 | 0 | 30 | 16,216.99 |
| 11 | 5,000 | 0 | 29 | 15,593.26 |
| 12 | 5,000 | 0 | 28 | 14,993.52 |
| 13 | 5,000 | 0 | 27 | 14,416.84 |
| 14 | 5,000 | 0 | 26 | 13,862.35 |
| 15 | 5,000 | 0 | 25 | 13,329.18 |
| 16 | 5,000 | 0 | 24 | 12,816.52 |
| 17 | 5,000 | 0 | 23 | 12,323.58 |
| 18 | 5,000 | 0 | 22 | 11,849.59 |
| 19 | 5,000 | 0 | 21 | 11,393.84 |
| 20 | 5,000 | $5,000 | 20 | 21,911.23 |
| 21 | 4,750 | 0 | 19 | 10,007.53 |
| 22 | 4,750 | $5,000 | 18 | 19,751.71 |
| 23 | 4,500 | 0 | 17 | 8,765.55 |
| 24 | 4,500 | $5,000 | 16 | 17,793.32 |
| 25 | 4,250 | 0 | 15 | 7,654.01 |
| 26 | 4,250 | $5,000 | 14 | 16,018.01 |
| 27 | 4,000 | 0 | 13 | 6,660.29 |
| 28 | 4,000 | $5,000 | 12 | 14,409.29 |
| 29 | 3,750 | 0 | 11 | 5,772.95 |
| 30 | 3,750 | $5,000 | 10 | 12,952.14 |
| 31 | 3,500 | 0 | 9 | 4,981.59 |
| 32 | 3,500 | $5,000 | 8 | 11,632.84 |
| 33 | 3,250 | 0 | 7 | 4,276.78 |
| 34 | 3,250 | $5,000 | 6 | 10,438.88 |
| 35 | 3,000 | 0 | 5 | 3,649.96 |
| 36 | 3,000 | $5,000 | 4 | 9,358.87 |
| 37 | 2,750 | 0 | 3 | 3,093.38 |
| 38 | 2,750 | $5,000 | 2 | 8,382.40 |
| 39 | 2,500 | 0 | 1 | 2,600.00 |
| 40 | 2,500 | $50,000 | 0 | 0 |
| | | | | $515,392.31 |

Thus, the percentage of TDR contributed by the three components are

$$P = (\$100,000 / \$560,392) \times 100 = 17.85\%$$
$$I = (\$172,500 / \$560,392) \times 100 = 30.78\%$$
$$IOI = (\$287,892 / \$560,392) \times 100 = \underline{51.37\%}$$
$$100.00\%$$

The IOI component is so high because not only is the interest reinvested, but also the principal returned to the investor when the bonds are called is reinvested at our assumed 8% reinvestment rate.

From the above chart, you can see that our original $100,000 investment has grown to $560,392 in 20 years. This represents an annual return of 9% overall. Thus, the forced periodic calls and the lower reinvestment rate have a dramatic effect on the yield the investor actually receives. For this reason, the effects of a sinking fund must be taken into account when you are considering purchasing or selling a bond.

## Average-Life Approximations

Another way (and a simpler way ) of approaching the yield calculation of a bond with a sinking fund is *first* to compute the average life of the bond and *then* to compute the yield to that average life.

The average life of a given bond issue is the weighted average maturity of all the bonds in the issue. This is calculated by first multiplying the number of bonds that mature per year by the year of maturity and arriving at a sum (see Table 7-6 on page 76). Once you have this sum, you divide it by the number of bonds in the issue and multiply by 100.

$$172,500 / 1,000,000 = 0.1725 \text{ years} \times 100 = 17.25$$

Thus, the average life of this bond issue is 17.25 years.

A single 10% corporate bond purchased at 100 that matured in 17.25 years would have an annual yield of 9% (assuming an 8% reinvestment rate).

*Table 7-6.* The Computation of Average Life.

| No. of Bonds That Mature Per Year x Year of Maturity = Total |
|---|
| 5,000 of the bonds mature in 20 years = 100,000 |
| 500 of the bonds mature in 19 years = 9,500 |
| 500 of the bonds mature in 18 years = 9,000 |
| 500 of the bonds mature in 17 years = 8,500 |
| 500 of the bonds mature in 16 years = 8,000 |
| 500 of the bonds mature in 15 years = 7,500 |
| 500 of the bonds mature in 14 years = 7,000 |
| 500 of the bonds mature in 13 years = 6,500 |
| 500 of the bonds mature in 12 years = 6,000 |
| 500 of the bonds mature in 11 years = 5,500 |
| 500 of the bonds mature in 10 years = 5,000 |
| 172,500 |

It stands to reason, therefore, that the entire issue of sinking-fund bonds described above, with an average maturity of 17.25 years, should have an average return of 9%. Of course, for any one bond in the sinking-fund issue described above, the return can be anywhere from 8.94% to 9.32%, depending on whether the bond is one of the first bonds called—or one of the bonds that is never called.

However, when a large number of the bonds are considered, the ones that are called early are *balanced* by the ones that are never called, and so the collective return of the bonds approaches the return of a bond that matures at exactly 17.25 years. The larger the number of bonds considered, the closer the return the investor actually receives is likely to be to the expected 9%.

# Chapter 8

# *Zero-Coupon Bonds*

A *Zero-Coupon Bond (ZCB)* is a bond that is originally sold at a discount to its face value. The difference between the price at which the investor acquires the bond and the price at which the investor disposes of the bond represents the investor's entire TDR (in lieu of interest and IOI payments). If the bond is bought at its original offering and is held to its maturity, then

$$TDR = \text{maturity value} - \text{offering price}$$

If the bond is bought and sold in the secondary market, then

$$TDR = \text{sale price} - \text{purchase price}$$

Thus the investor has only two cash flows to consider, one out and one in. This makes the yield calculation very simple.

Our usual formula for TDR is

$$TDR = P + I + IOI$$

For ZCBs, this simplifies to:

$$TDR = P$$

Of course, knowing an investment's TDR is of little value without considering the time period over which those dollars were accumulated. If you know the time element, it's a simple matter to calculate the YTM. Since there are no reinvestments of interest payments, the RCY is the same as the YTM.

Also, because there are no reinvestments, we can use the simplified formula:

$$\text{Purchase price} = \frac{\text{maturity value}}{(1 + i)^n}$$

where

$i$ = the RCY and YTM

$n$ = the number of compounding periods

*Note*: One convention for ZCBs is to assume annual compounding.

Thus, the market price of any ZCB is the bond's maturity value (or sales price) discounted by the bond's YTM on a *compounded basis* over the term of the investment. For example, a zero-coupon bond that matures in five years with a 6% YTM would have a price of:

$$PV = \frac{\text{face value}}{(1 + i)^n} = \frac{1000}{(1 + 0.06)^5} = \$747.26$$

As always, a second way of determining the price of a ZCB is by preparing a cash-flow table like the one in Table 8-1 (opposite).

Thus, a 5-year, zero-coupon bond that is priced to offer a 6% return would sell for $747.26.

***Table 8-1.*** *The Annual Value of a Zero-Coupon Bond As It Approaches Maturity.*

| Value of Bond at End of Period | Period No. | Rate Per Period | Value of Bond at Start of Period |
|---|---|---|---|
| $1000.00 | 5 | 6% | $943.40 |
| 943.40 | 4 | 6 | 890.00 |
| 942.60 | 3 | 6 | 839.62 |
| 915.14 | 2 | 6 | 792.09 |
| 888.48 | 1 | 6 | 747.26 |

As a ZCB approaches maturity it increases in value. However, it does not increase in value in equal annual jumps. Instead, the value is accreted over the life of the bond. Table 8-2 (see page 80) and Figure 8-1 (see page 81) show the path followed by a $1000 zero coupon with eight years to maturity that is priced to yield 16%.

The value of a ZCB accretes because the market value is computed as if the bond paid interest and that interest was compounded even though no interest is actually paid or compounded. Assuming market interest rates and the bond's credit quality remain constant, the ZCB will follow its original accretion path.

Of course, at any given time after the bond is purchased, the level of market interest rates or the bond's credit rating can change and thus the bond's market value can become higher or lower than the bond's theoretical accreted value. Thus, like coupon bonds, zeros can sell at a *premium* or at a *discount*, although in the case of ZCBs, these terms relate to the relationship between the market value of the bond and its accreted value instead of to its face value (as in the case of a coupon bond).

## Factors Which Affect the Prices of ZCBs

The factors that affect the market value of a coupon bond also affect the market value of ZCBs, namely, changes in market interest rates, changes in the credit quality of the bond, changes in the tax treatment of the bond, and changes in the "popularity" of the vehicle relative to other vehicles.

**Table 8-2.** The Price of the Bond on a Straight-Line and on an Accreted Basis.

| Year to Maturity | Straight Line | Accreted Basis |
|---|---|---|
| 8 | $ 305.03 | $ 305.03 |
| 7 | 391.90 | 353.83 |
| 6 | 478.78 | 410.10 |
| 5 | 565.65 | 473.11 |
| 4 | 652.53 | 552.29 |
| 3 | 739.40 | 640.66 |
| 2 | 826.28 | 743.16 |
| 1 | 913.15 | 862.07 |
| 0 | 1000.00 | 1000.00 |

## Market Interest Rates

As we discussed earlier, the lower the coupon, the greater the change in market value to a given change in interest rates, or, in other words, the lower the coupon, the higher the volatility. Since ZCBs have the lowest coupons possible, they are extremely volatile and, therefore, experience large changes in market value as a result of changing market interest rates.

Table 8-3 (see page 82) shows the effect that a sudden 5-point drop in market interest rates would have on the market value of the 8-year, 16% ZCB we used in the previous example. If market interest rates for comparable debt instruments dropped to 11%, the value of the ZCB would rise and would accrete along a different path.

Figure 8-2 (see page 82) shows that if interest rates dropped 5 points, the value of the bond would move from $473.11 to $593.45. This represents a $120.34 profit and a 25.44% increase in value.

## Credit Quality

A ZCB is always a riskier investment from a credit-risk point of view than a coupon bond from the same issuer with the same maturity. The reason for this is that a coupon bond makes regular in-

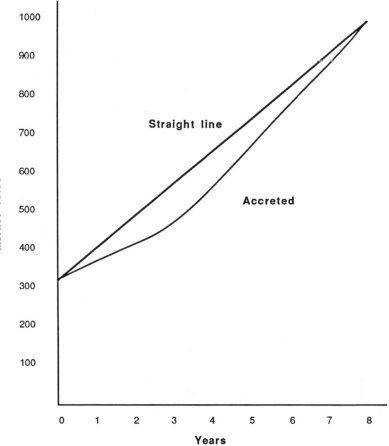

*Figure 8-1.*

**Table 8-3.** *Annual Values at Different Discount Rates.*

| Years to Maturity | 16% Interest Rate | 11% Interest Rate |
|:---:|:---:|:---:|
| 5 | $ 473.11 | $ 593.45 |
| 4 | 552.29 | 658.73 |
| 3 | 640.66 | 731.19 |
| 2 | 743.16 | 811.62 |
| 1 | 862.07 | 900.90 |
| 0 | 1000.00 | 1000.00 |

**Figure 8-2.**

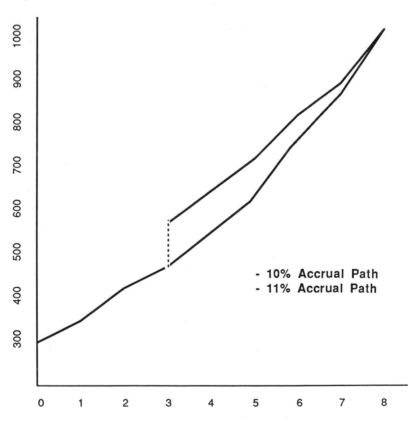

- 10% Accrual Path
- 11% Accrual Path

terest payments that reduce the amount of capital that the investor has at risk.

As an example, consider the case of an investor who has a choice between investing $10,000 in 30-year, 10% coupon bonds or $10,000 in 30-year, corporate ZCBs selling at a discount that yields the investor the same 10% YTM. If the investor elects to invest in the coupon bonds, she will receive, after just 7.5 years, interest and IOI payments that equal her original $10,000 investment.

Thus, if the bonds default after the 7.5-year mark, she will still have a positive rate of return on her investment (assuming, of course, that she reinvested her interest payments in a different bond that did not default).

If, however, she selects the ZCBs and, at *any time prior to their maturity*, they go into default, she will lose 100% of her principal, 100% of her imputed interest, and 100% of her imputed IOI.

If a ZCB has its credit rating upgraded or downgraded, the effect on its market value is also more dramatic than the effect that a similar change in credit rating has on a coupon bond. The reason for this is that when a ZCB is either upgraded or downgraded, not only is the credit rating of the principal and interest affected (as is the case with coupon bonds) but also the credit rating of the IOI payments.

## Tax Treatment

The tax treatment of the discount of ZCBs has changed several times over the last decade. It seems the IRS has had trouble deciding whether the normal accretion of a ZCB represents capital gains or interest income. Also, it took the IRS some time to decide whether to use straight-line amortization or accretion as the basis for taxation. As of 1987, the answers are "interest income" and "accretion," although many older ZCBs have been "grandfathered," with more attractive tax treatment. It's important to research the tax treatment of any ZCB before you buy or sell it.

## Popularity

Individual investment vehicles become popular or unpopular at different times for reasons that have nothing to do with the relative value of the investment—and ZCBs are no exception. For example, prior to the 1986 Tax Act, ZCBs were very attractive investment vehicles for Individual Retirement Accounts (IRAs). Now that the 1986 Tax Act has made IRAs less attractive for most taxpayers, fewer people are establishing IRAs and/or contributing to them. Therefore, there is less demand for ZCBs. Unless the supply of ZCBs also declines (through fewer offerings), we can expect that the yields of ZCBs will decline relative to the yields offered by coupon bonds simply as a result of the change in demand.

## Determining Yield

There are several ways of determining the yield of a ZCB, including:

1. by solving the PV/FV equation for the variable *i*
2. by trial and error
3. by looking up the bond in a book of bond tables
4. by using a $25 pocket calculator (by far the most popular option).

## Types of ZCBs

Corporations, municipalities, as well as the U.S. government and its agencies, have all issued zero-coupon instruments. Some examples of zero-coupon instruments are Treasury bills, Series EE U.S. savings bonds, and the whole collection of different "strip securities" (see discussion below).

## Why Issuers Elect Zero-Coupon Debt

ZCBs offer a way for issuers to borrow money for a fixed term without having to make periodic interest payments to the investors from whom they borrow. If a borrower wants to use the bond proceeds to build a new plant, for example, then financing with zeros makes sense. The new plant will not generate a positive cash flow for a number of years, and the debt used to finance it will not require servicing for a number of years—a convenient match.

Another reason an issuer might choose zero-coupon debt is that the issuer might be able to borrow money at a lower cost with zero-coupon than with non-zero-coupon debt. The reason is that investors might be willing to pay a premium for a zero-coupon security that does not expose them to reinvestment risk (more on this below).

## Why Investors Buy ZCBs

Investors buy ZCBs for a number of reasons, including convenience, the elimination of reinvestment risk, and as a "leveraged" trading vehicle.

### Convenience

From the point of view of convenience, ZCBs are tough to beat. You invest X number of dollars today and receive Y number of dollars at a fixed day in the future. For investors not familiar with the concepts of duration, immunization, and dedication (as they relate to bonds and bond-portfolio management), ZCBs provide a simple way to fund a specified and determinable future liability.

Thus, if an investor needs $10,000 a year for 4 consecutive years starting 10 years from today to fund a child's college education, the investor can buy 40 ZCBs today with maturities that coincide with his future liabilities (for example, 10 bonds maturing per year—starting in 10 years). So, for a fixed cost today, the investor can conveniently fund a future liability, *assuming he knows what that future liability will be.* This is a very important point because, if it turns out that college costs more than $10,000 a year in 10 years, then investing in these 40 ZCBs will obviously not fund this liability.

### Elimination of Reinvestment Risk

The second reason why zeros are popular is that they eliminate reinvestment risk. Since there are no reinvestments, there is no reinvestment risk. By choosing to invest in ZCBs instead of comparable coupon bonds, the investor eliminates reinvestment risk but increases exposure to credit risk and interest-rate risk. Credit risk can be eliminated by investing solely in U.S. government securities. This leaves only one risk: interest-rate risk. For this reason, U.S. government ZCBs are often considered to be a "pure interest-rate play."

In exchange for this "simplicity," the investor must accept a lower return. The yield of a U.S. government ACB is usually the lowest of any security with a comparable maturity.

Finally, for small investors, zeros offer the only practical way to earn a competitive return on a small investment. For example, if an investor purchases two coupon bonds at par (for his IRA) that yield 8% a year, then every six months the investor will receive $80 in interest. There are very few investment vehicles in which you can reinvest $80 and get a competitive return. Even money-market funds often have a $500 or $1000 minimum. Zeros solve the problem of how to reinvest small sums by automatically compounding the "coupons" internally.

## Leveraged Trading Vehicle

The third reason why investors invest in zeros is that they make excellent trading vehicles. Their high volatility, coupled with their liquidity (in the case of U.S. government zeros), make them ideal vehicles for interest-rate speculation. They are certainly simpler (although less leveraged) than bond futures or options on futures. Thus if an investor expects a decline in market interest rates, the investor would opt to buy ZCBs instead of coupon bonds in order to experience maximum capital appreciation.

As an illustration, Table 8-4 (opposite) compares the price changes of the following four bonds in response to a 3-point upward swing in market interest rates:

Bond 1—5-year, 9% coupon bond priced at par (YTM 9%)
Bond 2—5-year ZCB priced to yield 9%
Bond 3—30-year, 9% coupon bond priced at par (YTM 9%)
Bond 4—30-year ZCB priced to yield 9%

*Table 8-4.* The Change in Market Value of Different Bonds in Response to a 3-Point Change in Market Interest Rates.

| Bond No. | Price Before Swing | Price After Swing | Price Change ($) | Price Change (%) |
|----------|--------------------|--------------------|--------------------|--------------------|
| 1 | $1000.00 | $889.60 | 111.40 | 11.40 |
| 2 | 649.93 | 567.42 | 82.50 | 12.69 |
| 3 | 1000.00 | 757.58 | 242.22 | 24.22 |
| 4 | 75.37 | 33.37 | 41.99 | 55.71 |

Several conclusions can be drawn from Table 8-4:

1. For a given maturity and a given yield, a ZCB is much more re-sponsive to changes in market interest rates than is a coupon bond. This is logical, since coupon bonds have periodic pay-ments that can be reinvested at the higher rate available in the marketplace whereas the zero coupon has no cash flow that can be reinvested at a higher market rate. Therefore, while the re-sponse to a change in interest rates by the coupon bond can be made up partially by a change in market value and partially by a change in reinvestment income, for a ZCB the entire response must be made up by the change in market value of the bond. Hence the increase in volatility.

2. In response to changing interest rates, the change in price (ex-pressed as a percentage) for a short-term ZCB versus a longer-term ZCB is greater than for a short-term coupon bond versus a longer-term coupon bond. Again, this is due to the internal compounding of ZCBs. In the example used in Table 8-4, the difference in response to the change in market interest rates of the *5-year zero* as compared to the *30-year zero* is 43.02%. The difference in the responses of the two coupon bonds is only 12.82%.

*Table 8-5. Change in Price to Successive Changes in Yield.*

| Original Yield | Original Price | Final Yield | Final Price | Price Change (%) |
|---|---|---|---|---|
| 16% | $ 11.65 | 11% | $ 43.68 | 373.22 |
| 14 | 19.63 | 9 | 75.37 | 383.95 |
| 12 | 33.37 | 7 | 131.37 | 393.68 |
| 10 | 57.30 | 5 | 231.38 | 403.80 |
| 8 | 99.37 | 3 | 411.99 | 414.60 |
| 6 | 174.11 | 1 | 741.92 | 426.12 |

Table 8-5 above shows what happens to the market value of be-low-30-year U.S. government ZCBs if market interest rates drop by 5 points shortly after they are purchased.

In response to a 5-point swing in market interest rates, the bonds in Table 8-5, regardless of their initial yield, all appreciate about 400% without credit risk! With these kinds of returns available in the ZCB market, why risk your capital in junk bonds for a 14% return?

Of course, buying ZCBs in a margin account can dramatically in-crease the return from a ZCB investment.

### Duration of ZCBs

The duration of a ZCB is always equal to the bond's maturity. Why? Well, remember that a bond's *duration* is that point at which the bond is equally exposed to both interest-rate risk and reinvestment risk. Since ZCBs pay no interest, there is no interest to reinvest. Therefore there is no change in IOI to offset (either partially or total-ly) the interest-rate risk. Thus a ZCB is always exposed to interest-rate risk, and its duration is therefore equal to its maturity date. At no time other than its maturity date is the investor protected from an ad-verse move in market interest rates.

### Buying and Selling Zeros

Because these bonds sell at a discount—and often a large dis-count—it's extremely important to pay very close attention to the price you are paying for a given security. Some firms have a policy of charging a point ($10) commission on each bond sold. For a regular coupon bond selling for about $1000, this commission is only 1% of the purchase price. However, for a ZCB, this same $10 can represent a much higher percentage of the purchase price. It is therefore essential to check a number of dealers for prices before buying or selling a ZCB.

## Creating ZCBs from Coupon Bonds

*Want to make a 7% + return on your money per day* with only a minimum amount of risk? Buy 20-year U.S. government bonds and sell each of the bond's cash flows separately to investors with shorter time horizons. Since investors with shorter time horizons are willing to accept lower yields than those offered by 20-year bonds, you're able to sell the shorter-term cash flows for more than they cost you. The difference between your purchase price and your sales price (minus expenses and overhead) is pure profit.

For example, Figure 8-3 (see page 90) shows a typical yield curve for U.S. government coupon bonds. As you can see, shorter-term securities yield substantially less than do long-term bonds. According to this yield curve, the 20-year bonds are yielding 10%. If we were to buy 100 of these bonds at par, then every six months we would have a $5000 cash flow from the interest payments.

If we then lined up investors who wanted to invest in shorter-term U.S. government securities, we could sell those investors the future periodic $5000 interest payments at a discount that would give them the same yield that U.S. government securities of comparable maturity were yielding. Of course, we bought all the cash flows at a 10% discount, so when we resell them at a lower discount, we make a profit! This is referred to as *coupon stripping* and is very profitable. (See Table 8-6 on page 91.)

Thus the present value of the cash flows *we receive* is $100,000 and is equal to our purchase price because our cash flows are discounted by our YTM. Because we are selling the cash flows as if they were short-term securities, we can price them above our pur-

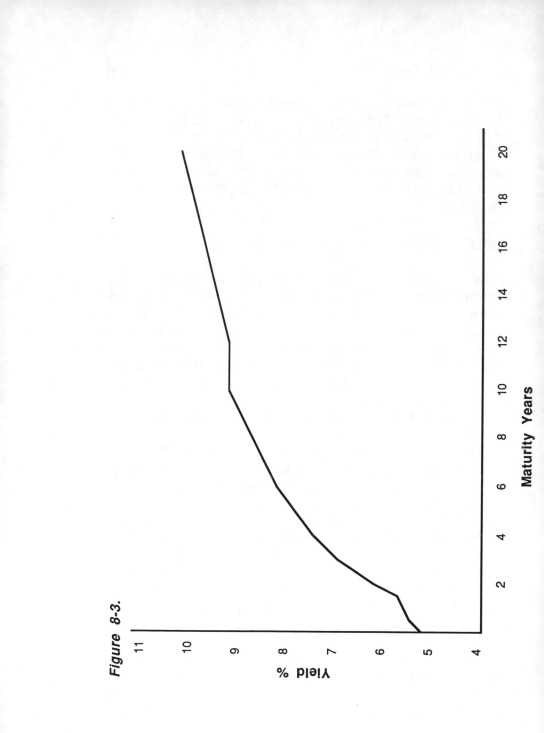

Figure 8-3.

**Table 8-6.** *The Present Values of the Future Cash Flows of $100,000 Worth of 20-Year Bonds Purchased at Par, Discounted at 10% and at the Current Term Interest Rate.*

| Maturity Months | | Market Yield | Sale Price of Cash Flow | Our Cost of Cash Flow | Our Profit |
|---|---|---|---|---|---|
| 6 | 1 | 5.5% | $ 4,866.18 | $ 4,761.90 | $ 104.28 |
| 12 | 2 | 5.7 | 4,726.74 | 4,535.15 | 191.59 |
| 18 | 3 | 5.9 | 4,595.76 | 4,319.18 | 276.58 |
| 24 | 4 | 6.1 | 4,433.82 | 4,113.51 | 320.31 |
| 30 | 5 | 6.6 | 4,250.78 | 3,917.63 | 333.15 |
| 36 | 6 | 7.0 | 4,067.50 | 3,731.07 | 336.43 |
| 42 | 7 | 7.3 | 3,890.32 | 3,553.41 | 336.91 |
| 48 | 8 | 7.6 | 3,710.15 | 3,384.20 | 325.95 |
| 54 | 9 | 7.8 | 3,543.48 | 3,223.04 | 320.44 |
| 60 | 10 | 8.0 | 3,377.82 | 3,069.57 | 308.25 |
| 66 | 11 | 8.1 | 3,230.78 | 2,923.40 | 307.38 |
| 72 | 12 | 8.2 | 3,087.18 | 2,784.19 | 302.99 |
| 78 | 13 | 8.3 | 2,947.13 | 2,651.61 | 295.52 |
| 84 | 14 | 8.4 | 2,810.75 | 2,525.34 | 285.41 |
| 90 | 15 | 8.5 | 2,678.11 | 2,405.09 | 273.02 |
| 96 | 16 | 8.6 | 2,549.30 | 2,290.56 | 258.74 |
| 102 | 17 | 8.8 | 2,404.70 | 2,181.48 | 223.22 |
| 108 | 18 | 8.9 | 2,283.59 | 2,077.60 | 205.99 |
| 114 | 19 | 8.9 | 2,186.30 | 1,978.67 | 207.63 |
| 120 | 20 | 9.0 | 2,073.21 | 1,884.45 | 188.76 |
| 126 | 21 | 9.0 | 1,983.94 | 1,794.71 | 189.23 |
| 132 | 22 | 9.1 | 1,878.63 | 1,709.25 | 169.38 |
| 138 | 23 | 9.1 | 1,796.87 | 1,627.86 | 169.01 |
| 144 | 24 | 9.2 | 1,699.06 | 1,550.34 | 148.72 |
| 150 | 25 | 9.2 | 1,624.34 | 1,476.51 | 147.83 |
| 156 | 26 | 9.3 | 1,533.73 | 1,406.20 | 127.53 |
| 162 | 27 | 9.3 | 1,465.58 | 1,339.24 | 126.34 |
| 168 | 28 | 9.4 | 1,381.86 | 1,275.47 | 106.39 |
| 174 | 29 | 9.4 | 1,319.82 | 1,214.73 | 105.09 |
| 180 | 30 | 9.5 | 1,242.65 | 1,156.89 | 85.76 |
| 186 | 31 | 9.5 | 1,186.30 | 1,101.80 | 84.50 |
| 192 | 32 | 9.6 | 1,115.34 | 1,049.33 | 66.01 |
| 198 | 33 | 9.6 | 1,064.26 | 999.36 | 64.90 |
| 204 | 34 | 9.7 | 999.18 | 951.77 | 47.41 |
| 210 | 35 | 9.7 | 952.96 | 906.45 | 46.51 |
| 216 | 36 | 9.8 | 893.41 | 863.29 | 30.12 |
| 222 | 37 | 9.8 | 851.68 | 822.18 | 29.50 |
| 228 | 38 | 9.9 | 797.33 | 783.03 | 14.30 |
| 234 | 39 | 9.9 | 759.72 | 745.74 | 13.98 |
| 240 | 40 | 10.0 | 14,914.80 | 14,914.80 | 00.00 |
| | | | $107,175.06 | $100,000.00 | $7,175.06 |

chase price so as to yield the lower yields of shorter-term securities and have a present value profit of $7,175.06 *per day for every $100,000 worth of ZCBs we create* (minus expenses, of course).

To guarantee that the cash flows are paid to the investors, we would place the bonds into a trust account held for the benefit of the investors. Only the profits would be distributed to the investment banking firm.

U.S. BONDS ⟶ TRUST COMPANY ⸺ $$$ ⟶ INVESTOR

⸺ $$$ ⟶ INVESTMENT BANKER

## Callable Zeros

Some ZCBs are also callable. ZCBs that are callable fall into two categories: (1) those that are callable any time after a brief period of call protection and (2) those that have a long period of call protection and are only callable late in their life (for example, the last five years). Bonds in the second category are often referred to as *tail bonds*.

For bonds that are callable at any time, the call price is usually a fixed percentage over the bond's accreted value—such as 103% of the bond's accreted value (the accreted value in this case being the accreted value assuming the bond's original offering rate). Because of the high volatility of these bonds, it's important to keep close track of the call features of the bond. Buying a ZCB at a high premium over its accreted value only to have it called shortly thereafter can be heart- (and wallet) breaking. A bond that is callable is also limited in its appreciation potential because any potential purchaser (at least any informed one) will take the call provisions into account when deciding what price to bid for it.

## Chapter 9

# Convertible Bonds

For purposes of this chapter, *convertible bonds (CBs)* are "bonds that are convertible into a fixed number of shares of the company's common stock." This definition distinguishes these bonds from another type of bond that we will call *exchangeable bonds,* which are defined as "bonds that are convertible from one type of debt instrument to another."

Investors who purchase CBs can profit in a number of different ways:

1. from capital appreciation stemming from an increase in the market value of the underlying common stock
2. from interest (and IOI) income that the bond generates
3. from the amortization of any discount as the bond approaches maturity
4. from capital appreciation in the value of the bond due to a drop in market interest rates.

Because so many factors affect the market value of a convertible bond, it is more difficult to analyze than is a straight bond. For that reason, let's begin with a brief review.

## Background

Convertible bonds are usually convertible into a fixed number of shares of a company's common stock at any time at the option of the investor. Since the bond can be converted into a fixed number of the company's common stock, the price of the bond rises as the price of the stock rises.

For example, let's assume that a hypothetical company—ABC Manufacturing—issues a convertible bond at par with a 9% coupon that's convertible into 100 shares of the company's common stock. At the time the bond is issued, ABC Manufacturing's common stock is selling for $8 a share and pays no dividend.

If an investor buys this bond and immediately converts it into common stock, the investor is converting a $1000 bond into $800 worth of common stock. This means the Conversion Value (CV) of the bond at the time it is issued is $800. If the market value of the stock rises, so does the conversion value, and vice versa. In other words:

CV = the no. of shares of stock that a bond can be converted into

     x   the current price per share

   = no. of shares x current share price

If the market value of the stock rises to $15 per share, the CV of the bond rises to $1500. This makes the bond worth at least $1500 because it can be converted into $1500 worth of common stock. Actually, however, the bond is worth more than $1500 because:

1. The bond generates $90 a year of interest, whereas the stock does not generate any dividend income.
2. The bond, by being senior to the common stock, is less risky in the event of bankruptcy.

3. The bond is exposed to less market risk in that the stream of coupon payments establishes a floor for the price of the bond (barring a default). Thus, even if the value of the company's stock drops to $0.50 per share, the value of the bond does not drop below the value of nonconvertible debt instruments with the same credit rating and maturity.

4. The bond matures and returns the investor's capital at a definite point in the future (again barring a default); the stock comes with no such guarantee.

For all of these reasons, CBs generally trade at a premium to their conversion value. The answer to the question of how much of a premium is justifiable varies from bond to bond and investor to investor. In fact, trying to answer this question is the focus of most CB analysis.

## Calculating Conversion Price and Conversion Premium

In order to analyze the conversion premium, we must be able to calculate it accurately. In the above example, the initial Conversion Premium (CP) is 25% and is determined by the following formula:

$$\frac{\text{Purchase Price}}{\text{No. of Shares the Bond Converts into}} = \text{Conversion Price}$$

$$\frac{\$1000}{100} = \$10$$

The CP (expressed as a percentage), therefore, would be

$$\frac{\text{Conversion Price} - \text{Market Price}}{\text{Market Price}} = \frac{\$10 - \$8}{\$8} \times 100 = 25\%$$

This means that the value of the stock has to rise *by 25% before the CV of the bond will be equal to the bond's purchase price.* The

CP changes constantly because investors are constantly evaluating and reevaluating the relative attractiveness of the CB and the stock.

The question that any potential investor in a convertible must consider, therefore, is, "Given the current CP of the CB, is the CB a better buy than the stock, or is the stock a better buy than the CB?"

## Factors Which Affect the Size of the Premium and Therefore the Choice Between the Convertible Bond and the Stock

The size of the premium depends on a variety of factors.

1. Which way does the investor expect interest rates to move? If the investor expects interest rates to drop, then buying the CB in expectation of a capital gain due to a decline in market interest rates makes sense. In this case, the investor might be tempted to pay a higher premium for a CB.

2. What is the spread between the bond's yield to maturity and the stock's dividend return? The higher this yield spread is, the more attractive the bond becomes relative to the stock. To quantify the relative attractiveness of different stock/bond yield spreads, the spread between the bond's yield and the stock's yield is often compared to the size of the CP.

The way these two factors are compared is by calculating the *workout period*, which is defined as "the number of years it will take for the extra yield that the bond pays to equal the CP."

For the bond in our example, the workout period equals

$$\frac{\text{CP in Dollars}}{\text{No. of Dollars the Bond Pays per Year} - \text{No. of Dollars the Stock Pays per Year}} = \frac{\$200}{\$90 - 0} = 2.22 \text{ years}$$

Thus, if the investor buys the CB, then the investor will collect enough interest over the first 2.22 years to equal the CP. Naturally, the lower the workout period, the more attractive the CB relative to the stock. Many investors also use workout periods to compare the relative attractiveness of different CBs.

For example, if Convertible Bond A has a workout period of two years, and Convertible Bond B has a workout period of six years, then Bond A is a better buy relative to Stock A than Bond B is to Stock B. Also, if both bonds offer about the same yield and both companies have approximately the same growth potential, then Bond A is also probably a better buy than Bond B.

A more precise calculation of a CB's workout period would also consider the amount of earned IOI as well as the amount of simple interest. In the above example, the time required for the semiannual $45 interest payments (compounding at a 9% reinvestment rate) to equal the $200 CP would be only 2 years (instead of 2.2 years) if the IOI is included in the calculation.

The shorter the workout period, the sooner the investor receives enough additional income from the bond to reimburse the investor for the premium that the bond costs. Thus a high premium can be offset in a short period of time by a high yield spread. Thus you need to consider the yield spread between the stock and the bond, not only on an absolute basis but also on a relative basis as compared to the size of the CP.

3. What is the size of the increase expected in the stock's market value, and what is the time frame over which this increase is expected to occur? If the stock's market value rises substantially and quickly, then investing in the stock is the better option. However, if the stock's market value rises slowly (or not at all), then the CB is a better investment. Thus, the *longer* the time frame over which the investor expects the stock to rise, the higher the premium the investor should be willing to pay to own the bond instead of the stock.

Again using the above bond as an example, if the investor expects the market value of the stock to rise by 2 points over a *one-year* period, then a $1000 stock investment will yield the following *annualized* return:

125 shares x $2 profit per share = $250 = *25% per year*

A $1000 bond investment, on the other hand, would yield an annualized return of 100 shares multiplied by $10 per share. This would equal a $1000 CV plus $90 in interest and $2 in IOI over the year for a total return of $92. However, we would also need to include an estimate of the CP in our calculation. If we assume that the bond trades at a 10% CP, then the value of the bond would be

$$CV \times (1 + CP) + I + IOI = TDR$$

where

$$I = \text{the interest}$$
$$IOI = \text{the interest on interest}$$

$$\$1000 \times (1 + 0.1) + \$90 + \$2 = \$1192$$
$$= \text{an } 11.92\% \text{ annualized return}$$

However, if the price of the stock rises 5 points over a *10-year* period, then a $1000 stock investment would yield the following annualized return:

$$125 \text{ shares} \times \$5 \text{ profit per share} = \$625$$
$$= 6.25\% \text{ per year}$$

A $1000 bond investment, on the other hand, would yield an annualized return of (assuming a 10% CP):

$$CV \times (1 + .CP) + I + IOI = TDR$$
$$\$1300 \times (1 + 0.10) + \$900 + \$511.71 = \$2841.71$$
$$= \text{an } 11.01\% \text{ annualized return}$$

Thus the bond would clearly be a better investment choice than the company's common stock.

4. What is the company's underlying financial strength? If a company is weak financially (many emerging-growth companies and turn-around situations fall into this category), the bond becomes more attractive than the stock. If the company goes bankrupt, an investor is much better off if he owns the company's bonds than if he owns the company's stock.

For example, let's compare the return that an investor in the bond receives with what an investor in the stock receives if the company goes bankrupt five years after a $1000 investment.

If you invested in the stock, you would probably have a 100% loss. However, if you invested in the CBs, you would have already received $450 in interest ($90 per year for five years) and $102.97 of IOI for a total dollar return of $552.97. Thus your loss would be limited to 44.7%. Also, if there were any assets left after the secured creditors were paid off, you might receive some additional return from the bankruptcy courts.

Thus an investor who is worried about a company's financial strength will be willing to pay a higher premium in order to own the CBs instead of the common stock.

5. What are the investor's investment objectives and tolerance for risk? If the investor's investment objectives are balanced and the investor has a low tolerance for risk, then the investor will be willing to pay a higher premium in order to own the CB instead of the stock. If, however, the investor's objectives are to maximize capital gains, then the investor will only be interested in CBs that have a relatively low CP.

# Chapter 10

# Mortgage-Backed Securities

Analyzing and predicting the yields of Mortgage-Backed Securities (MBSs) is more complex than analyzing straight bonds because the securities themselves are more complex. MBSs not only have more cash flows, but there is also more uncertainty about when those cash flows will be received. Because calculating the RCY and TDR of an MBS is more complex than calculating these factors for a garden-variety bond, we will first review why and how MBSs came into existence. Hopefully, after we have discussed why MBSs came into existence, you will find the calculations involved in predicting their yields to be more sensible.

## Background

At one time, local savings and loans and other financial institutions originated mortgages in their local markets, held the mortgages in their investment portfolios (i.e., as assets on their balance sheets), serviced the mortgages (collected the monthly payments, and so on), and accrued to their income statements any profits or losses that resulted from making the mortgage loans.

While this way of doing mortgage business was very profitable when interest rates were stable, it created real problems for the issuing institutions when interest rates became more volatile. The reason that volatile interest rates caused problems for institutions that originated and held mortgage loans is that this approach frequently resulted in a mismatch of assets and liabilities.

Savings and loans institutions raise money by offering savings accounts, NOW accounts, checking accounts, and short-term certificates of deposit, all of which are sources of short-term funds. Mortgage loans, on the other hand, are long-term loans (30 years being the most popular term). Thus institutions that make mortgage loans often borrow short-term funds and then relend those funds at a higher long-term interest rate.

If, for example, a financial institution can borrow money at 6% by offering certificates of deposit to investors, it can lend money to home buyers at 9%, initially making a 3-point spread over its cost of funds. However if, as time passes, interest rates go up sharply, the financial institution may find itself paying 12% to borrow money via its short-term sources of funds (certificates of deposit, NOW accounts and so on) in order to support a 9% outstanding mortgage loan that it made several years ago. This means that the institution could be losing 3 points per year on this mortgage loan. The dramatic increase in short-term interest rates in the late 1970s and early 1980s caught many financial institutions in this type of an asset/liability mismatch. This mismatch was, in turn, a major reason why a record number of savings and loans institutions closed (and are still closing) their doors.

In response to this problem, mortgage institutions looked for ways to mitigate the risk of asset/liability mismatches. The solutions they devised took two principal forms:

1. issuing adjustable-rate mortgages
2. securitizing mortgage loans.

## Adjustable-Rate Mortgages

An Adjustable-Rate Mortgage (ARM) differs from a traditional mortgage in that the interest rate that the home owner is charged is periodically adjusted to reflect market interest rates. Interest rates on mortgage loans can thus be adjusted up and down in line with the institution's cost of funds; when the bank has to pay more to its depositors to attract funds, it can pass those higher costs on to the home owners and thus maintain its "positive yield spread."

However, because of limitations on how much the interest rate charged on a given mortgage can be increased over a one-year period (usually 2%) and over the life of the mortgage loan (usually 5%), the ARM does not provide the institution with a perfect hedge. Also, differences between when the bank's cost of funds increases and when it can pass those increases on to home owners also weaken the hedge offered by an ARM.

Besides not being a perfect hedge, ARMs also have problems from a marketing point of view. Borrowers, except for those who have difficulty qualifying for a mortgage, have shown a clear preference for traditional fixed-rate mortgages. Thus ARMs are not the ideal answer to mortgage institutions' asset/liability mismatch problem.

## Securitizing Mortgages

The second alternative available to a mortgage institution is to sell the mortgages it originates to investors. By doing this, the financial institution can keep the lucrative mortgage-origination fees, the very profitable mortgage-servicing business, and transfer both the interest-rate risk *and* the credit risk on to the investor.

If the institution can sell the mortgage as soon as it is issued, then the institution can "recycle its capital." The institution can then use that capital to make another mortgage loan, earn another origination fee, and add another mortgage to its lucrative servicing business.

However, selling individual mortgages is difficult. They are an unattractive investment to many investors for the following reasons:

1. There is a high minimum investment. Most individual mortgages are many thousands of dollars in size, much too large for the average investor.

2. Mortgage loans are often made in unusual amounts (i.e., $83,765.34), which makes them cumbersome and unattractive to many investors.

3. It is difficult to assess the credit risk involved. Most investors lack the time, resources, and expertise to do the property appraisals, employment verifications, credit checks, and so on that are necessary to accurately assess the credit risk inherent in an individual mortgage.

4. There is no ready market for individual mortgages. Thus an investor who purchases a mortgage and later wants to resell it may have a problem reselling it quickly at a fair price.

5. There are accounting headaches. A traditional mortgage is a self-amortizing investment. This means that each monthly payment is part principal and part interest. Adding to the complexity is the fact that the percentage of each varies from month to month. An MBS is also a self-liquidating investment in that the investor receives his principal back as part of the monthly payments. The self-liquidating nature of MBSs makes many investors uncomfortable with them.

6. There are prepayment problems. Almost all mortgages can be prepaid by the borrower at any time without penalty, and so the investor in an MBS can never be sure of his investment's "maturity."

For these reasons, a well-developed liquid market for individual mortgages never really developed until the mortgage institutions started securitizing their mortgage portfolios. *Securitizing mortgages* means taking individual mortgages and turning them into readily marketable securities that are easy to analyze and trade.

The securitization process begins when an institution sells mortgages to a sophisticated financial intermediary. By selling the mortgage to the intermediary, the institution effectively recycles its capital.

**Participation Certificates.** The intermediary then combines various mortgages into pools and resells *undivided* interests in the pools to investors (just as the owner of a co-op apartment buys a percentage interest in the whole building). These undivided interests are called *Participating Certificates (PCs)*. The intermediary then receives the mortgage payments from the home owners (via the servicing organizations) and passes them through to investors on a proportional basis. The intermediary also guarantees investors that if any of the underlying mortgages goes into default, the intermediary will pay the investors all the principal and interest to which they are entitled.

By having the intermediaries create these certificates, institutions solved several of the problems associated with investing in individual mortgages. For example:

1. The minimum investment was reduced to $25,000. The creation of numerous mutual funds that invest in these participation certificates made it possible for investors to participate in this market with minimum investments as low as $1000.

2. These mutual funds allowed investors to invest any amount of money (over the minimum) in this market. No longer were investors limited to irregular investment sums.

3. The investor did not have to check credit ratings of home owners. The intermediary performed all the necessary credit checks and backed up its work by guaranteeing all of the mortgages it used to back its PCs. Thus, from the investor's point of view, the credit strength of the PC comes not from the home owner and the property involved but from the credit strength of the intermediary. This is probably the biggest advantage that investing in PCs offers relative to investing in individual mortgages.

4. After these PCs started to be issued in large numbers, a very liquid market developed. Today they are some of the most liquid securities available.

However pooling individual mortgages into PCs did not solve all of the problems associated with investing in mortgages. For example:

1. The accounting problem is not solved in that both principal and interest are still passed through to the investors on a monthly basis, and the percentage of each changes from month to month. PCs are also self-liquidating.

2. The prepayment problem is also not solved in that the underlying mortgages can still be prepaid at any time; so the investor still does not really know what the weighted maturity of the underlying mortgage portfolio will be.

**Collateralized Mortgage Obligations.** A Collateralized Mortgage Obligation (CMO) goes one step further than a PC. In a CMO offering, the intermediary again buys a portfolio of individual mortgages, but instead of combining the mortgages into pools and selling participating interests in those pools, the intermediary uses the mortgages as collateral for a more traditional bond offering (i.e., bonds that pay their interest every six months and return all their principal at maturity).

The bonds that are issued as a CMO are generally issued in different "tranches," or classes. There are usually between three and five classes per offering. The classes differ with respect to their *interest rates* and *maximum maturity* dates.

When the yield curve is positively sloped, the class of bonds with the shortest maximum maturity (usually called *Class A bonds*) offers the lowest coupon. Each subsequent class has a longer maximum maturity and a higher coupon. For example, if an intermediary assembled a $1,000,000,000 portfolio of mortgages yielding 10%, it might structure a CMO offering so that it included five classes of bonds, each with a $200,000,000 face amount but with the following yields and average maturities:

Class A: yielding  8.0%—to be fully paid off in 3 years
Class B: yielding  8.5%—to be fully paid off in 6 years
Class C: yielding  9.0%—to be fully paid off in 12 years
Class D: yielding  9.5%—to be fully paid off in 20 years
Class E: yielding 10.0%—to be fully paid off in 30 years

These CMOs would pay their investors interest only every six months like a traditional bond. There would be no monthly payments of principal. This makes the accounting easier than the accounting for PCs.

Instead, all of the principal (both the regular principal that is paid as part of the mortgages' amortization and any principal repayments) is first used to pay off the Class A bonds. After the Class A bonds are fully retired, the principal is then applied to retiring the Class B bonds, and so on.

Although the different classes have so-called maximum maturities, most, if not all, of the bonds in a given class are usually retired prior to their maximum maturity date. The maximum maturity date is calculated by assuming that there are no prepayments of principal and thus the only source of principal with which to retire the bonds is the normal amortization of the mortgages.

Investing in a given class of CMOs has two advantages over investing in a PC: (1) the accounting is simpler and (2) the investor has more control over the maturity of his investment.

In exchange for this control and simplicity, investors who purchase bonds in the shorter-term CMO classes accept a lower yield then they would receive from a PC.

## The Major Intermediaries

There are three major intermediaries that package individual mortgages and resell them as PCs and CMOs:

1. The Government National Mortgage Association (GNMA) buys pools of VA-guaranteed and FHA-insured mortgage loans. Both the principal and interest of GNMA securities are backed by the full faith and credit of the U.S. government. The securities offered by the GNMA are commonly referred to as *Ginnie Maes*. The Government National Mortgage Association is part of the federal system that encourages and supports home ownership.

2. The Federal Home Loan Mortgage Corporation (FHLMC) buys conventional mortgages that are not guaranteed by the VA or FHA. The FHLMC guarantees the timely payment of interest and the ultimate payment of principal. The securities issued by the FHLMC are commonly referred to as *Freddie Macs*. The Federal Home Loan Mortgage Corporation is also part of the federal system that encourages and supports home ownership.

3. The Federal National Mortgage Association (FNMA) buys a variety of mortgages from lenders and reoffers them to investors. The FNMA used to be a government agency but was sold to the public and is now one of the largest publicly traded corporations listed on the New York Stock Exchange. Securities offered by FNMA are commonly referred to as *Fannie Maes*.

In addition, many of the larger mortgage companies and investment banking firms sell mortgage securities under their own names with private insurance backing.

## Analyzing Yields of Mortgage-Backed Securities

Just as with every other type of interest-bearing security, the three components that make up the TDR of a mortgage security are principal, interest and IOI. Unfortunately, that's where the similarity with traditional bonds ends.

With a traditional bond—corporate, municipal, or government— you know when the bond will mature. Even if the bond is subject to call options, put features, or a sinking fund, it's still possible to derive a reasonably accurate maturity schedule so that the bond can be compared to other investment options in the marketplace.

Analyzing mortgage securities, however, is more complex. This is because so many variables and complications need to be taken into account. Let's examine some of the many variables that affect the TDR of PCs and CMOs.

## Analyzing PCs

### Principal Component

Because of the high credit ratings and tremendous financial strength of the major financial intermediaries, there is little question that the investor will, eventually, receive his principal (i.e., there is little credit risk). However *when* the investor will receive his principal is another question.

Principal is paid to the investor from one of two sources: (1) normal amortization of the underlying mortgages and (2) principal prepayments.

Normal-amortization principal is the principal component of the monthly payments that the various home owners make. For most mortgages (and thus most mortgage securities), the amortization schedule is such that in the early years, most of the payments made by home owners are interest, and most of the later payments are principal. This creates a problem because even though the regular monthly payments are in equal installments, the percentage of interest to principal varies from payment to payment (see Table 10-1 on pages 110-119).

An investor who purchased the mortgage illustrated in Table 10-1 right after it was first issued would receive only a small amount of principal back in the first five years. However, if that investor bought the mortgage when it had only five years left, the principal component of the monthly payments would be very high.

Since interest is paid only on the remaining balance, this has no effect on the security's interest component, only on the amount of regular principal that's returned per month. Thus if there were no prepayments, the amount of principal that the investor received per month would steadily increase over the term of the security. However, there is a second way in which the investor's principal may be returned.

The second way principal may be returned to investors is through principal prepayments.

**Table 10-1.** The Amortization Schedule of a $100,000, 10%, 30-Year Mortgage.

| Month | Payment | Interest | Principal | Remaining Balance |
|-------|---------|----------|-----------|-------------------|
| 1 | $877.58 | $833.33 | $44.25 | $99,955.75 |
| 2 | 877.58 | 832.96 | 44.62 | 99,911.13 |
| 3 | 877.58 | 832.59 | 44.99 | 99,866.15 |
| 4 | 877.58 | 832.22 | 45.36 | 99,820.79 |
| 5 | 877.58 | 831.84 | 45.74 | 99,775.05 |
| 6 | 877.58 | 831.46 | 46.12 | 99,728.92 |
| 7 | 877.58 | 831.07 | 46.51 | 99,682.42 |
| 8 | 877.58 | 830.69 | 46.89 | 99,635.53 |
| 9 | 877.58 | 830.30 | 47.28 | 99,588.24 |
| 10 | 877.58 | 829.90 | 47.68 | 99,540.56 |
| 11 | 877.58 | 829.50 | 48.08 | 99,492.49 |
| 12 | 877.58 | 829.10 | 48.48 | 99,444.01 |
| 13 | 877.58 | 828.70 | 48.88 | 99,395.13 |
| 14 | 877.58 | 828.29 | 49.29 | 99,345.84 |
| 15 | 877.58 | 827.88 | 49.70 | 99,296.15 |
| 16 | 877.58 | 827.47 | 50.11 | 99,246.03 |
| 17 | 877.58 | 827.05 | 50.53 | 99,195.50 |
| 18 | 877.58 | 826.63 | 50.95 | 99,144.55 |
| 19 | 877.58 | 826.20 | 51.38 | 99,093.18 |
| 20 | 877.58 | 825.78 | 51.80 | 99,041.38 |
| 21 | 877.58 | 825.34 | 52.24 | 98,989.14 |
| 22 | 877.58 | 824.91 | 52.67 | 98,936.47 |
| 23 | 877.58 | 824.47 | 53.11 | 98,883.36 |
| 24 | 877.58 | 824.03 | 53.55 | 98,829.81 |
| 25 | 877.58 | 823.58 | 54.00 | 98,775.81 |
| 26 | 877.58 | 823.13 | 54.45 | 98,721.36 |
| 27 | 877.58 | 822.68 | 54.90 | 98,666.46 |
| 28 | 877.58 | 822.22 | 55.36 | 98,611.10 |
| 29 | 877.58 | 821.76 | 55.82 | 98,555.28 |
| 30 | 877.58 | 821.29 | 56.29 | 98,498.99 |
| 31 | 877.58 | 820.82 | 56.76 | 98,442.24 |
| 32 | 877.58 | 820.35 | 57.23 | 98,385.01 |
| 33 | 877.58 | 819.88 | 57.70 | 98,327.31 |
| 34 | 877.58 | 819.39 | 58.19 | 98,269.12 |
| 35 | 877.58 | 818.91 | 58.67 | 98,210.45 |
| 36 | 877.58 | 818.42 | 59.16 | 98,151.29 |
| 37 | 877.58 | 817.93 | 59.65 | 98,091.64 |
| 38 | 877.58 | 817.43 | 60.15 | 98,031.49 |

*Table 10-1. (Cont.)*

| Month | Payment | Interest | Principal | Remaining Balance |
|-------|---------|----------|-----------|-------------------|
| 39 | 877.58 | 816.93 | 60.65 | 97,970.84 |
| 40 | 877.58 | 816.42 | 61.16 | 97,909.68 |
| 41 | 877.58 | 815.91 | 61.67 | 97,848.01 |
| 42 | 877.58 | 815.40 | 62.18 | 97,785.83 |
| 43 | 877.58 | 814.88 | 62.70 | 97,723.14 |
| 44 | 877.58 | 814.36 | 63.22 | 97,659.92 |
| 45 | 877.58 | 813.83 | 63.75 | 97,596.17 |
| 46 | 877.58 | 813.30 | 64.28 | 97,531.89 |
| 47 | 877.58 | 812.77 | 64.81 | 97,467.07 |
| 48 | 877.58 | 812.23 | 65.35 | 97,401.72 |
| 49 | 877.58 | 811.68 | 65.90 | 97,335.82 |
| 50 | 877.58 | 811.13 | 66.45 | 97,269.37 |
| 51 | 877.58 | 810.58 | 67.00 | 97,202.37 |
| 52 | 877.58 | 810.02 | 67.56 | 97,134.81 |
| 53 | 877.58 | 809.46 | 68.12 | 97,066.69 |
| 54 | 877.58 | 808.89 | 68.69 | 96,998.00 |
| 55 | 877.58 | 808.32 | 69.26 | 96,928.73 |
| 56 | 877.58 | 807.74 | 69.84 | 96,858.89 |
| 57 | 877.58 | 807.16 | 70.42 | 96,788.47 |
| 58 | 877.58 | 806.57 | 71.01 | 96,717.46 |
| 59 | 877.58 | 805.98 | 71.60 | 96,645.86 |
| 60 | 877.58 | 805.38 | 72.20 | 96,573.66 |
| 61 | 877.58 | 804.78 | 72.80 | 96,500.86 |
| 62 | 877.58 | 804.17 | 73.41 | 96,427.46 |
| 63 | 877.58 | 803.56 | 74.02 | 96,353.44 |
| 64 | 877.58 | 802.95 | 74.63 | 96,278.80 |
| 65 | 877.58 | 802.32 | 75.26 | 96,203.55 |
| 66 | 877.58 | 801.70 | 75.88 | 96,127.66 |
| 67 | 877.58 | 801.06 | 76.52 | 96,051.15 |
| 68 | 877.58 | 800.43 | 77.15 | 95,973.99 |
| 69 | 877.58 | 799.78 | 77.80 | 95,896.20 |
| 70 | 877.58 | 799.13 | 78.45 | 95,817.75 |
| 71 | 877.58 | 798.48 | 79.10 | 95,738.65 |
| 72 | 877.58 | 797.82 | 79.76 | 95,658.90 |
| 73 | 877.58 | 797.16 | 80.42 | 95,578.47 |
| 74 | 877.58 | 796.49 | 81.09 | 95,497.38 |
| 75 | 877.58 | 795.81 | 81.77 | 95,415.61 |
| 76 | 877.58 | 795.13 | 82.45 | 95,333.16 |

*Table* *10-1.* (Cont.)

| Month | Payment | Interest | Principal | Remaining Balance |
|-------|---------|----------|-----------|-------------------|
| 77 | 877.58 | 794.44 | 83.14 | 95,250.02 |
| 78 | 877.58 | 793.75 | 83.83 | 95,166.19 |
| 79 | 877.58 | 793.05 | 84.53 | 95,081.67 |
| 80 | 877.58 | 792.35 | 85.23 | 94,996.43 |
| 81 | 877.58 | 791.64 | 85.94 | 94,910.49 |
| 82 | 877.58 | 790.92 | 86.66 | 94,823.83 |
| 83 | 877.58 | 790.20 | 87.38 | 94,736.45 |
| 84 | 877.58 | 789.47 | 88.11 | 94,648.34 |
| 85 | 877.58 | 788.74 | 88.84 | 94,559.50 |
| 86 | 877.58 | 788.00 | 89.58 | 94,469.91 |
| 87 | 877.58 | 787.25 | 90.33 | 94,379.58 |
| 88 | 877.58 | 786.50 | 91.08 | 94,288.50 |
| 89 | 877.58 | 785.74 | 91.84 | 94,196.66 |
| 90 | 877.58 | 784.97 | 92.61 | 94,104.05 |
| 91 | 877.58 | 784.20 | 93.38 | 94,010.67 |
| 92 | 877.58 | 783.42 | 94.16 | 93,916.51 |
| 93 | 877.58 | 782.64 | 94.94 | 93,821.57 |
| 94 | 877.58 | 781.85 | 95.73 | 93,725.83 |
| 95 | 877.58 | 781.05 | 96.53 | 93,629.30 |
| 96 | 877.58 | 780.24 | 97.34 | 93,531.97 |
| 97 | 877.58 | 779.43 | 98.15 | 93,433.82 |
| 98 | 877.58 | 778.62 | 98.96 | 93,334.86 |
| 99 | 877.58 | 777.79 | 99.79 | 93,235.07 |
| 100 | 877.58 | 776.96 | 100.62 | 93,134.44 |
| 101 | 877.58 | 776.12 | 101.46 | 93,032.99 |
| 102 | 877.58 | 775.27 | 102.31 | 92,930.68 |
| 103 | 877.58 | 774.42 | 103.16 | 92,827.52 |
| 104 | 877.58 | 773.56 | 104.02 | 92,723.51 |
| 105 | 877.58 | 772.70 | 104.88 | 92,618.62 |
| 106 | 877.58 | 771.82 | 105.76 | 92,512.86 |
| 107 | 877.58 | 770.94 | 106.64 | 92,406.22 |
| 108 | 877.58 | 770.05 | 107.53 | 92,298.70 |
| 109 | 877.58 | 769.16 | 108.42 | 92,190.27 |
| 110 | 877.58 | 768.25 | 109.33 | 92,080.94 |
| 111 | 877.58 | 767.34 | 110.24 | 91,970.70 |
| 112 | 877.58 | 766.42 | 111.16 | 91,859.55 |
| 113 | 877.58 | 765.50 | 112.08 | 91,747.46 |
| 114 | 877.58 | 764.56 | 113.02 | 91,634.45 |

*Table* *10-1.* *(Cont.)*

| Month | Payment | Interest | Principal | Remaining Balance |
|-------|---------|----------|-----------|-------------------|
| 115 | 877.58 | 763.62 | 113.96 | 91,520.49 |
| 116 | 877.58 | 762.67 | 114.91 | 91,405.58 |
| 117 | 877.58 | 761.71 | 115.87 | 91,289.71 |
| 118 | 877.58 | 760.75 | 116.83 | 91,172.88 |
| 119 | 877.58 | 759.77 | 117.81 | 91,055.07 |
| 120 | 877.58 | 758.79 | 118.79 | 90,936.28 |
| 121 | 877.58 | 757.80 | 119.78 | 90,816.51 |
| 122 | 877.58 | 756.80 | 120.78 | 90,695.73 |
| 123 | 877.58 | 755.80 | 121.78 | 90,573.95 |
| 124 | 877.58 | 754.78 | 122.80 | 90,451.15 |
| 125 | 877.58 | 753.76 | 123.82 | 90,327.33 |
| 126 | 877.58 | 752.73 | 124.85 | 90,202.48 |
| 127 | 877.58 | 751.69 | 125.89 | 90,076.59 |
| 128 | 877.58 | 750.64 | 126.94 | 89,949.64 |
| 129 | 877.58 | 749.58 | 128.00 | 89,821.64 |
| 130 | 877.58 | 748.51 | 129.07 | 89,692.58 |
| 131 | 877.58 | 747.44 | 130.14 | 89,562.44 |
| 132 | 877.58 | 746.35 | 131.23 | 89,431.21 |
| 133 | 877.58 | 745.26 | 132.32 | 89,298.89 |
| 134 | 877.58 | 744.16 | 133.42 | 89,165.47 |
| 135 | 877.58 | 743.05 | 134.53 | 89,030.93 |
| 136 | 877.58 | 741.92 | 135.66 | 88,895.28 |
| 137 | 877.58 | 740.79 | 136.79 | 88,758.49 |
| 138 | 877.58 | 739.65 | 137.93 | 88,620.57 |
| 139 | 877.58 | 738.50 | 139.08 | 88,481.49 |
| 140 | 877.58 | 737.35 | 140.23 | 88,341.26 |
| 141 | 877.58 | 736.18 | 141.40 | 88,199.85 |
| 142 | 877.58 | 735.00 | 142.58 | 88,057.27 |
| 143 | 877.58 | 733.81 | 143.77 | 87,913.50 |
| 144 | 877.58 | 732.61 | 144.97 | 87,768.53 |
| 145 | 877.58 | 731.40 | 146.18 | 87,622.36 |
| 146 | 877.58 | 730.19 | 147.39 | 87,474.97 |
| 147 | 877.58 | 728.96 | 148.62 | 87,326.34 |
| 148 | 877.58 | 727.72 | 149.86 | 87,176.48 |
| 149 | 877.58 | 726.47 | 151.11 | 87,025.37 |
| 150 | 877.58 | 725.21 | 152.37 | 86,873.01 |
| 151 | 877.58 | 723.94 | 153.64 | 86,719.37 |
| 152 | 877.58 | 722.66 | 154.92 | 86,564.45 |

*Table* *10-1.* *(Cont.)*

| Month | Payment | Interest | Principal | Remaining Balance |
|-------|---------|----------|-----------|-------------------|
| 153 | 877.58 | 721.37 | 156.21 | 86,408.24 |
| 154 | 877.58 | 720.07 | 157.51 | 86,250.73 |
| 155 | 877.58 | 718.76 | 158.82 | 86,091.90 |
| 156 | 877.58 | 717.43 | 160.15 | 85,931.76 |
| 157 | 877.58 | 716.10 | 161.48 | 85,770.27 |
| 158 | 877.58 | 714.75 | 162.83 | 85,607.45 |
| 159 | 877.58 | 713.40 | 164.18 | 85,443.26 |
| 160 | 877.58 | 712.03 | 165.55 | 85,277.71 |
| 161 | 877.58 | 710.65 | 166.93 | 85,110.78 |
| 162 | 877.58 | 709.26 | 168.32 | 84,942.45 |
| 163 | 877.58 | 707.85 | 169.73 | 84,772.73 |
| 164 | 877.58 | 706.44 | 171.14 | 84,601.59 |
| 165 | 877.58 | 705.01 | 172.57 | 84,429.02 |
| 166 | 877.58 | 703.58 | 174.00 | 84,255.01 |
| 167 | 877.58 | 702.13 | 175.45 | 84,079.56 |
| 168 | 877.58 | 700.66 | 176.92 | 83,902.64 |
| 169 | 877.58 | 699.19 | 178.39 | 83,724.25 |
| 170 | 877.58 | 697.70 | 179.88 | 83,544.37 |
| 171 | 877.58 | 696.20 | 181.38 | 83,363.00 |
| 172 | 877.58 | 694.69 | 182.89 | 83,180.11 |
| 173 | 877.58 | 693.17 | 184.41 | 82,995.70 |
| 174 | 877.58 | 691.63 | 185.95 | 82,809.75 |
| 175 | 877.58 | 690.08 | 187.50 | 82,622.25 |
| 176 | 877.58 | 688.52 | 189.06 | 82,433.19 |
| 177 | 877.58 | 686.94 | 190.64 | 82,242.55 |
| 178 | 877.58 | 685.35 | 192.23 | 82,050.32 |
| 179 | 877.58 | 683.75 | 193.83 | 81,856.50 |
| 180 | 877.58 | 682.14 | 195.44 | 81,661.05 |
| 181 | 877.58 | 680.51 | 197.07 | 81,463.98 |
| 182 | 877.58 | 678.87 | 198.71 | 81,265.27 |
| 183 | 877.58 | 677.21 | 200.37 | 81,064.90 |
| 184 | 877.58 | 675.54 | 202.04 | 80,862.86 |
| 185 | 877.58 | 673.86 | 203.72 | 80,659.14 |
| 186 | 877.58 | 672.16 | 205.42 | 80,453.72 |
| 187 | 877.58 | 670.45 | 207.13 | 80,246.59 |
| 188 | 877.58 | 668.72 | 208.86 | 80,037.73 |
| 189 | 877.58 | 666.98 | 210.60 | 79,827.13 |
| 190 | 877.58 | 665.23 | 212.35 | 79,614.77 |

*Table* 10-1. *(Cont.)*

| Month | Payment | Interest | Principal | Remaining Balance |
|-------|---------|----------|-----------|-------------------|
| 191 | 877.58 | 663.46 | 214.12 | 79,400.65 |
| 192 | 877.58 | 661.67 | 215.91 | 79,184.74 |
| 193 | 877.58 | 659.87 | 217.71 | 78,967.04 |
| 194 | 877.58 | 658.06 | 219.52 | 78,747.51 |
| 195 | 877.58 | 656.23 | 221.35 | 78,526.16 |
| 196 | 877.58 | 654.38 | 223.20 | 78,302.97 |
| 197 | 877.58 | 652.52 | 225.06 | 78,077.91 |
| 198 | 877.58 | 650.65 | 226.93 | 77,850.98 |
| 199 | 877.58 | 648.76 | 228.82 | 77,622.16 |
| 200 | 877.58 | 646.85 | 230.73 | 77,391.43 |
| 201 | 877.58 | 644.93 | 232.65 | 77,158.78 |
| 202 | 877.58 | 642.99 | 234.59 | 76,924.19 |
| 203 | 877.58 | 641.03 | 236.55 | 76,687.64 |
| 204 | 877.58 | 639.06 | 238.52 | 76,449.13 |
| 205 | 877.58 | 637.08 | 240.50 | 76,208.62 |
| 206 | 877.58 | 635.07 | 242.51 | 75,966.12 |
| 207 | 877.58 | 633.05 | 244.53 | 75,721.59 |
| 208 | 877.58 | 631.01 | 246.57 | 75,475.02 |
| 209 | 877.58 | 628.96 | 248.62 | 75,226.40 |
| 210 | 877.58 | 626.89 | 250.69 | 74,975.71 |
| 211 | 877.58 | 624.80 | 252.78 | 74,722.92 |
| 212 | 877.58 | 622.69 | 254.89 | 74,468.03 |
| 213 | 877.58 | 620.57 | 257.01 | 74,211.02 |
| 214 | 877.58 | 618.43 | 259.15 | 73,951.87 |
| 215 | 877.58 | 616.27 | 261.31 | 73,690.55 |
| 216 | 877.58 | 614.09 | 263.49 | 73,427.06 |
| 217 | 877.58 | 611.89 | 265.69 | 73,161.37 |
| 218 | 877.58 | 609.68 | 267.90 | 72,893.47 |
| 219 | 877.58 | 607.45 | 270.13 | 72,623.34 |
| 220 | 877.58 | 605.19 | 272.39 | 72,350.95 |
| 221 | 877.58 | 602.92 | 274.66 | 72,076.29 |
| 222 | 877.58 | 600.64 | 276.94 | 71,799.35 |
| 223 | 877.58 | 598.33 | 279.25 | 71,520.10 |
| 224 | 877.58 | 596.00 | 281.58 | 71,238.52 |
| 225 | 877.58 | 593.65 | 283.93 | 70,954.59 |
| 226 | 877.58 | 591.29 | 286.29 | 70,668.30 |
| 227 | 877.58 | 588.90 | 288.68 | 70,379.62 |
| 228 | 877.58 | 586.50 | 291.08 | 70,088.54 |

*Table* *10-1.* *(Cont.)*

| Month | Payment | Interest | Principal | Remaining Balance |
|-------|---------|----------|-----------|-------------------|
| 229 | 877.58 | 584.07 | 293.51 | 69,795.03 |
| 230 | 877.58 | 581.63 | 295.95 | 69,499.08 |
| 231 | 877.58 | 579.16 | 298.42 | 69,200.66 |
| 232 | 877.58 | 576.67 | 300.91 | 68,899.75 |
| 233 | 877.58 | 574.16 | 303.42 | 68,596.33 |
| 234 | 877.58 | 571.64 | 305.94 | 68,290.39 |
| 235 | 877.58 | 569.09 | 308.49 | 67,981.90 |
| 236 | 877.58 | 566.52 | 311.06 | 67,670.83 |
| 237 | 877.58 | 563.92 | 313.66 | 67,357.18 |
| 238 | 877.58 | 561.31 | 316.27 | 67,040.91 |
| 239 | 877.58 | 558.67 | 318.91 | 66,722.00 |
| 240 | 877.58 | 556.02 | 321.56 | 66,400.44 |
| 241 | 877.58 | 553.34 | 324.24 | 66,076.19 |
| 242 | 877.58 | 550.63 | 326.95 | 65,749.25 |
| 243 | 877.58 | 547.91 | 329.67 | 65,419.58 |
| 244 | 877.58 | 545.16 | 332.42 | 65,087.16 |
| 245 | 877.58 | 542.39 | 335.19 | 64,751.97 |
| 246 | 877.58 | 539.60 | 337.98 | 64,413.99 |
| 247 | 877.58 | 536.78 | 340.80 | 64,073.20 |
| 248 | 877.58 | 533.94 | 343.64 | 63,729.56 |
| 249 | 877.58 | 531.08 | 346.50 | 63,383.06 |
| 250 | 877.58 | 528.19 | 349.39 | 63,033.67 |
| 251 | 877.58 | 525.28 | 352.30 | 62,681.37 |
| 252 | 877.58 | 522.34 | 355.24 | 62,326.14 |
| 253 | 877.58 | 519.38 | 358.20 | 61,967.94 |
| 254 | 877.58 | 516.40 | 361.18 | 61,606.76 |
| 255 | 877.58 | 513.39 | 364.19 | 61,242.57 |
| 256 | 877.58 | 510.35 | 367.23 | 60,875.35 |
| 257 | 877.58 | 507.29 | 370.29 | 60,505.06 |
| 258 | 877.58 | 504.21 | 373.37 | 60,131.69 |
| 259 | 877.58 | 501.10 | 376.48 | 59,755.21 |
| 260 | 877.58 | 497.96 | 379.62 | 59,375.59 |
| 261 | 877.58 | 494.80 | 382.78 | 58,992.80 |
| 262 | 877.58 | 491.61 | 385.97 | 58,606.83 |
| 263 | 877.58 | 488.39 | 389.19 | 58,217.64 |
| 264 | 877.58 | 485.15 | 392.43 | 57,825.21 |
| 265 | 877.58 | 481.88 | 395.70 | 57,429.50 |
| 266 | 877.58 | 478.58 | 399.00 | 57,030.50 |

*Table* *10-1.* *(Cont.)*

| Month | Payment | Interest | Principal | Remaining Balance |
|-------|---------|----------|-----------|-------------------|
| 267 | 877.58 | 475.25 | 402.33 | 56,628.18 |
| 268 | 877.58 | 471.90 | 405.68 | 56,222.50 |
| 269 | 877.58 | 468.52 | 409.06 | 55,813.44 |
| 270 | 877.58 | 465.11 | 412.47 | 55,400.97 |
| 271 | 877.58 | 461.67 | 415.91 | 54,985.07 |
| 272 | 877.58 | 458.21 | 419.37 | 54,565.70 |
| 273 | 877.58 | 454.71 | 422.87 | 54,142.83 |
| 274 | 877.58 | 451.19 | 426.39 | 53,716.44 |
| 275 | 877.58 | 447.64 | 429.94 | 53,286.50 |
| 276 | 877.58 | 444.05 | 433.53 | 52,852.97 |
| 277 | 877.58 | 440.44 | 437.14 | 52,415.83 |
| 278 | 877.58 | 436.80 | 440.78 | 51,975.05 |
| 279 | 877.58 | 433.13 | 444.45 | 51,530.60 |
| 280 | 877.58 | 429.42 | 448.16 | 51,082.44 |
| 281 | 877.58 | 425.69 | 451.89 | 50,630.55 |
| 282 | 877.58 | 421.92 | 455.66 | 50,174.89 |
| 283 | 877.58 | 418.12 | 459.46 | 49,715.43 |
| 284 | 877.58 | 414.30 | 463.28 | 49,252.15 |
| 285 | 877.58 | 410.43 | 467.15 | 48,785.00 |
| 286 | 877.58 | 406.54 | 471.04 | 48,313.96 |
| 287 | 877.58 | 402.62 | 474.96 | 47,839.00 |
| 288 | 877.58 | 398.66 | 478.92 | 47,360.08 |
| 289 | 877.58 | 394.67 | 482.91 | 46,877.16 |
| 290 | 877.58 | 390.64 | 486.94 | 46,390.23 |
| 291 | 877.58 | 386.59 | 490.99 | 45,899.23 |
| 292 | 877.58 | 382.49 | 495.09 | 45,404.15 |
| 293 | 877.58 | 378.37 | 499.21 | 44,904.93 |
| 294 | 877.58 | 374.21 | 503.37 | 44,401.56 |
| 295 | 877.58 | 370.01 | 507.57 | 43,894.00 |
| 296 | 877.58 | 365.78 | 511.80 | 43,382.20 |
| 297 | 877.58 | 361.52 | 516.06 | 42,866.14 |
| 298 | 877.58 | 357.22 | 520.36 | 42,345.77 |
| 299 | 877.58 | 352.88 | 524.70 | 41,821.08 |
| 300 | 877.58 | 348.51 | 529.07 | 41,292.00 |
| 301 | 877.58 | 344.10 | 533.48 | 40,758.52 |
| 302 | 877.58 | 339.65 | 537.93 | 40,220.60 |
| 303 | 877.58 | 335.17 | 542.41 | 39,678.19 |
| 304 | 877.58 | 330.65 | 546.93 | 39,131.26 |

*Table 10-1. (Cont.)*

| Month | Payment | Interest | Principal | Remaining Balance |
|-------|---------|----------|-----------|-------------------|
| 305 | 877.58 | 326.09 | 551.49 | 38,579.78 |
| 306 | 877.58 | 321.50 | 556.08 | 38,023.69 |
| 307 | 877.58 | 316.86 | 560.72 | 37,462.98 |
| 308 | 877.58 | 312.19 | 565.39 | 36,897.59 |
| 309 | 877.58 | 307.48 | 570.10 | 36,327.49 |
| 310 | 877.58 | 302.73 | 574.85 | 35,752.64 |
| 311 | 877.58 | 297.94 | 579.64 | 35,173.00 |
| 312 | 877.58 | 293.11 | 584.47 | 34,588.53 |
| 313 | 877.58 | 288.24 | 589.34 | 33,999.18 |
| 314 | 877.58 | 283.33 | 594.25 | 33,404.93 |
| 315 | 877.58 | 278.37 | 599.21 | 32,805.72 |
| 316 | 877.58 | 273.38 | 604.20 | 32,201.53 |
| 317 | 877.58 | 268.35 | 609.23 | 31,592.29 |
| 318 | 877.58 | 263.27 | 614.31 | 30,977.98 |
| 319 | 877.58 | 258.15 | 619.43 | 30,358.55 |
| 320 | 877.58 | 252.99 | 624.59 | 29,733.96 |
| 321 | 877.58 | 247.78 | 629.80 | 29,104.16 |
| 322 | 877.58 | 242.53 | 635.05 | 28,469.12 |
| 323 | 877.58 | 237.24 | 640.34 | 27,828.78 |
| 324 | 877.58 | 231.91 | 645.67 | 27,183.11 |
| 325 | 877.58 | 226.53 | 651.05 | 26,532.05 |
| 326 | 877.58 | 221.10 | 656.48 | 25,875.57 |
| 327 | 877.58 | 215.63 | 661.95 | 25,213.62 |
| 328 | 877.58 | 210.11 | 667.47 | 24,546.16 |
| 329 | 877.58 | 204.55 | 673.03 | 23,873.13 |
| 330 | 877.58 | 198.94 | 678.64 | 23,194.49 |
| 331 | 877.58 | 193.29 | 684.29 | 22,510.20 |
| 332 | 877.58 | 187.58 | 690.00 | 21,820.20 |
| 333 | 877.58 | 181.84 | 695.74 | 21,124.46 |
| 334 | 877.58 | 176.04 | 701.54 | 20,422.91 |
| 335 | 877.58 | 170.19 | 707.39 | 19,715.52 |
| 336 | 877.58 | 164.30 | 713.28 | 19,002.24 |
| 337 | 877.58 | 158.35 | 719.23 | 18,283.01 |
| 338 | 877.58 | 152.36 | 725.22 | 17,557.79 |
| 339 | 877.58 | 146.31 | 731.27 | 16,826.53 |
| 340 | 877.58 | 140.22 | 737.36 | 16,089.17 |
| 341 | 877.58 | 134.08 | 743.50 | 15,345.66 |
| 342 | 877.58 | 127.88 | 749.70 | 14,595.96 |

*Table 10-1.* *(Cont.)*

| Month | Payment | Interest | Principal | Remaining Balance |
|-------|---------|----------|-----------|-------------------|
| 343 | 877.58 | 121.63 | 755.95 | 13,840.02 |
| 344 | 877.58 | 115.33 | 762.25 | 13,077.77 |
| 345 | 877.58 | 108.98 | 768.60 | 12,309.17 |
| 346 | 877.58 | 102.58 | 775.00 | 11,534.17 |
| 347 | 877.58 | 96.12 | 781.46 | 10,752.71 |
| 348 | 877.58 | 89.61 | 787.97 | 9,964.73 |
| 349 | 877.58 | 83.04 | 794.54 | 9,170.19 |
| 350 | 877.58 | 76.42 | 801.16 | 8,369.03 |
| 351 | 877.58 | 69.74 | 807.84 | 7,561.19 |
| 352 | 877.58 | 63.01 | 814.57 | 6,746.62 |
| 353 | 877.58 | 56.22 | 821.36 | 5,925.26 |
| 354 | 877.58 | 49.38 | 828.20 | 5,097.06 |
| 355 | 877.58 | 42.48 | 835.10 | 4,261.96 |
| 356 | 877.58 | 35.52 | 842.06 | 3,419.89 |
| 357 | 877.58 | 28.50 | 849.08 | 2,570.81 |
| 358 | 877.58 | 21.42 | 856.16 | 1,714.66 |
| 359 | 877.58 | 14.29 | 863.29 | 851.36 |
| 360 | 877.58 | 7.09 | 870.49 | − 19.12 |

In the United States, almost all mortgages can be prepaid without penalty. In effect, then, almost all home owners with mortgages have a put option with regard to their mortgages that is exercisable at any time. Home owners choose to exercise their put options for a variety of reasons, including:

1. The home owner wants to pay off the mortgage for nonfinancial reasons. Many Americans still get a tremendous sense of satisfaction from "burning the mortgage" and make paying off their mortgages a high financial priority.
2. The home owner sells the home either to move to a different home in the same area or to move out of the area. When a home owner sells his home, the balance of his mortgage must be paid off with the sales proceeds (unless it is an assumable mortgage).

3. The home owner refinances. When interest rates drop sharply, there is a financial incentive for the home owner to refinance his mortgage at a lower interest rate. However, the new rate must be low enough to more than offset the costs of refinancing—including points on the new mortgage, appraisal fees, application fees, and so on—for refinancing to be attractive.

Intermediaries may also occasionally pay off one of the mortgages in a pool in which investors own interests. They may do this when a home owner defaults on his mortgage. Thus prepayment rates also depend upon the default rate. In turn, default rates for a given pool of mortgages depend upon a whole variety of national and regional economic factors. (Try building a spread sheet that includes all of these variables and you'll soon understand the problem of accurately predicting the prepayment rates of a given pool of mortgages.)

## Conventions For Expressing Prepayment Rates. Due
to the combined effects of the above factors, few mortgages actually run for their full 30-year terms. Since most mortgages are prepaid, it would be very inaccurate to compute mortgage yields based on 30-year maturities. Even if a mortgage runs for its full 30 years, most of the principal is returned to the investor prior to the home owner's final payment. If the reinvestment rate is different from the PC's yield (as it almost always is), using a 30-year maturity to compute the PC's yield would be invalid.

Instead, the standard convention is to quote mortgage securities yields based on various prepayment assumptions.

## 12-Year Assumption. One of the most commonly used conventions is to assume that all of the mortgages backing a given PC will be paid off in 12 years. In other words, for yield-calculation purposes, it is assumed that a mortgage will prepay none of its principal prior to the 12-year point and then it will prepay all of its principal.

Naturally, if we're considering only one mortgage, this 12-year assumption is ludicrous because any one mortgage can have a term as short as 1 month or as long as 30 years.

But the 12-year assumption is reasonable when we consider a pool of mortgages as a single security. With a well-diversified portfolio, the theory is that the mortgages that are paid off early will be offset by the mortgages that run for a longer term, in effect balancing the portfolio's average life at around the 12-year mark. (See Chapter 7, on sinking funds, for a more detailed discussion of average life.)

Twelve years was selected as the convention because historically, FHA mortgages have had a 12-year average life. Unfortunately, the historical data on prepayments is of limited value because the data was assembled during a period of relative stability in interest rates. Despite periodic updates, this data still lags substantially behind the market's true results. As of this date, the average pool's maturity is much shorter than 12 years.

The dramatic interest-rate swings we've experienced over the last few years have played such havoc with the 12-year assumption that yields for mortgage securities are now often analyzed assuming different prepayment rates based upon the PC's coupon rate and the current market interest rate (although PCs are still often quoted on a 12-year basis).

**Percentage-of-FHA Experience.** If a given PC closely follows the FHA historical prepayment schedule, the pool is said to *prepay at 100% of FHA experience*. A graphical representation of a mortgage paying off at 100% of FHA experience would look like Figure 10-1 (see page 122). Note that half of the principal is repaid by the 125th month (instead of the 283rd month without any prepayments).

If a given PC prepays three times as fast as the historical norm, the pool is said to *prepay at 300% of FHA experience*, and the average life of the pool shortens accordingly. Naturally, if a mortgage prepays at half of the FHA historical rate, it is said to *prepay at 50% of historical performance*, and the average life lengthens. Figure 10-2 (see page 122) shows how various *paydown speeds* affect the schedule by which principal is repaid to investors.

**Fixed-Prepayment Assumption.** A second convention that's often used is to assume that a fixed percentage of the remaining

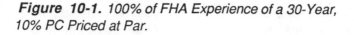

**Figure 10-1.** *100% of FHA Experience of a 30-Year, 10% PC Priced at Par.*

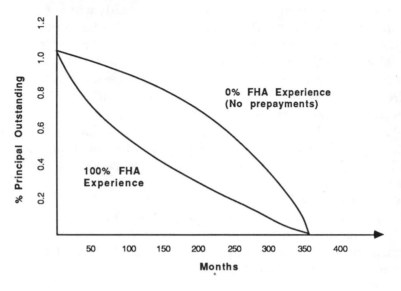

**Figure 10-2.**

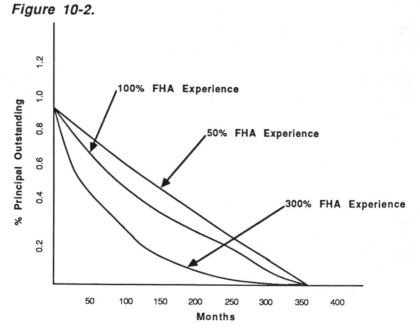

122

principal repays each month. If you are considering only one mortgage at a time, this makes no sense because the mortgage is either paid off or not paid off in a given month (thus the prepayment rate for an individual mortgage for a given month is either 100% or 0). However, the greater the number of mortgages in the pool, the more valid this assumption becomes.

For example, if, historically, 1% of a large pool of mortgages has been paid off each month, the pool has a prepayment rate of 1%. The prepayment rate will probably stay near 1% over the near term, but not over the long term.

*Regardless of which convention you use to express repayment speed, you must keep in mind that the speed at which different PCs prepay principal changes over time.* Thus the fact that a mortgage has prepaid at 300% of FHA experience over the last five years does not mean that it will continue to do so in the future. A prepayment "track record" is of limited value when used as a tool to predict a PC's future prepayment rate.

At any time, a given PC's remaining balance is equal to its FV (future value) multiplied by the percentage of principal not yet repaid. For example, if a $100,000 PC had 65% of its principal repaid to date, the remaining balance would be

$$\$100,000 \times 0.35 = \$35,000$$

(The actual percentage of principal not yet repaid for each pool for each month is available from the various intermediaries in both hard copy and on-line form and is updated monthly.)

## Interest Component

The interest component is determined by multiplying the principal amount by the coupon rate. Since the amount of principal changes each month, this calculation has to be done on a monthly basis, using either the actual (or the expected) amount of principal remaining for each month and multiplying it by the prorated interest rate for the month. This calculation is very similar to the one for a sinking-fund bond (see Chapter 7).

## *IOI Component*

The IOI component is the sum of the monthly cash flows compounded at the assumed reinvestment rate for the number of compounding periods.

$$\text{IOI} = \text{monthly cash flows} \times (1 + i)^n$$

where

monthly cash flow = (principal prepayments + interest + amortized
principal for each month)

$i$ = assumed reinvestment rate per period

$n$ = number of compounding periods

Since the monthly cash flow can only be "guesstimated," any prediction of the IOI component can also only be guesstimated.

**The Relationship Between Coupon, Paydown Speed, and RCY.** The way in which a given PC's coupon interacts with changing market interest rates to alter the security's RCY is very different from the way these variables interact for traditional bonds. With traditional bonds, changing market interest rates affect the IOI component but do not affect either the principal or the interest component of a bond's TDR (assuming the bond is held to maturity).

However, with PCs, a change in market interest rates not only affects the reinvestment rate and thus the IOI component but also affects the prepayment rate, which, in turn, increases or decreases the PC's average life and thus also affects the interest component.

In general, if market interest rates go down, the rate of prepayment increases because home owners move to refinance their mortgages at the lower interest rates. Thus as market interest rates go down, the average life of the security decreases. This means that the investor will get more principal back in a shorter period of time *just when the investor least wants to receive it.* There are two reasons why the accelerated return of principal works to the disadvantage of the investor.

1. When the investor receives principal back, it has to be reinvested at the lower market interest rate then available, thus reducing the IOI component.
2. The principal is no longer invested at the higher yield at which the security was originally purchased, thus reducing the interest component.

However, if market interest rates go up, home owners are in no hurry to prepay their mortgages because they have more attractive investment opportunities elsewhere. Thus as market interest rates go up, the average life of an MBS increases. This means the investor is receiving less principal at a slower rate just when the investor would most like to have all his principal back. Again, this works to the disadvantage of the investor in two ways.

1. The principal cannot be reinvested at the then higher market rates, thus reducing the potential IOI component.
2. The principal remains invested at the lower rate at which the security was purchased, thus reducing the interest component.

Thus because the *home owners* have the put option, home owners have a larger degree of control over the investor's TDR and RCY. From the *investor's* point of view, PCs lack a put feature but yet are subject at any time to being called away at par.

By affecting the interest and the IOI factors simultaneously, a given change in market interest rates has a greater effect on the RCY of a PC than it has on the RCY of a traditional bond.

To illustrate, compute the RCY and TDR for a 10%, 12-year corporate bond and a 12-year GNMA for both a 10% and a 5% assumed reinvestment rate.

You can see that two of the principal factors affecting the RCY of a PC are the prepayment rate and the reinvestment rate. And since the prepayment rate is itself largely dependent upon changes in market interest rates, the overriding factor is really future market interest rates. Of course we never know what these rates will be, so we are severely limited in our ability to make RCY projections.

If, however, we assume a future market interest rate, we can predict a prepayment rate from up-to-date historical data. Once we assume a prepayment rate, we can calculate an expected return.

## Analyzing CMOs

Although simpler, CMOs pose their own obstacles to accurate analysis. Again, the term of the bond is largely dependent upon the prepayment rate which is, in turn, largely dependent upon future market interest rates.

If, for example, the market interest rate is 3 points *below* the coupon of the mortgages in the pool backing our CMO, then in order to derive an expected maturity schedule, we must first examine the historical data. We must look at this data in order to see what the historic prepayment rate is when the spread between mortgage interest rates and current interest rates is 3%. If we find that historically, there is a 2% prepayment rate when the mortgage/market interest rate spread is 3%, then we can assume a 2% prepayment rate again. This assumption will not be exact, but it should be fairly accurate.

Once we have a prepayment assumption, we can adjust the amortization schedule of the underlying mortgages to include the 2% prepayments per month. From this adjusted amortization schedule, we can easily calculate the total amount of principal returned at the end of each month. Once we know when principal will be returned, we can calculate the average life of the different classes of bonds in our CMO offering. Finally, from the average life, we can compute the estimated RCY and TDR of the different classes. For example, let's assume our CMO classes discussed earlier are backed by a $100,000 pool of 10%, 30-year mortgages. The calculation of estimated RCY and TDR (assuming the bonds can be called and retired on the coupon payment dates) is shown in Table 10-2 (see pages 127–133).

**Table 10-2.** Amortization Schedule Adjusted to Include 2% Prepayments.

| Month | Payment | Interest | Principal | Remaining Balance | 2% Prepay | Principal |
|---|---|---|---|---|---|---|
| 1 | $877.58 | $833.33 | $44.25 | $99,955.75 | $97,956.64 | $2,043.37 |
| 2 | 877.58 | 832.96 | 44.62 | 99,911.13 | 95,953.78 | 4,046.22 |
| 3 | 877.58 | 832.59 | 44.99 | 99,866.15 | 93,990.62 | 6,009.38 |
| 4 | 877.58 | 832.22 | 45.36 | 99,820.79 | 92,066.35 | 7,933.65 |
| 5 | 877.58 | 831.84 | 45.74 | 99,775.05 | 90,180.20 | 9,819.80 |
| 6 | 877.58 | 831.46 | 46.12 | 99,728.92 | 88,331.39 | 11,668.61 |
| 7 | 877.58 | 831.07 | 46.51 | 99,682.42 | 86,519.19 | 13,480.81 |
| 8 | 877.58 | 830.69 | 46.89 | 99,635.53 | 84,742.85 | 15,257.15 |
| 9 | 877.58 | 830.30 | 47.28 | 99,588.24 | 83,001.66 | 16,998.34 |
| 10 | 877.58 | 829.90 | 47.68 | 99,540.56 | 81,294.90 | 18,705.10 |
| 11 | 877.58 | 829.50 | 48.08 | 99,492.49 | 79,621.89 | 20,378.11 |
| 12 | 877.58 | 829.10 | 48.48 | 99,444.01 | 77,981.94 | 22,018.06 |
| 13 | 877.58 | 828.70 | 48.88 | 99,395.13 | 76,374.40 | 23,625.60 |
| 14 | 877.58 | 828.29 | 49.29 | 99,345.84 | 74,798.61 | 25,201.39 |
| 15 | 877.58 | 827.88 | 49.70 | 99,296.15 | 73,253.94 | 26,746.06 |
| 16 | 877.58 | 827.47 | 50.11 | 99,246.03 | 71,739.75 | 28,260.25 |
| 17 | 877.58 | 827.05 | 50.53 | 99,195.50 | 70,255.43 | 29,744.57 |
| 18 | 877.58 | 826.63 | 50.95 | 99,144.55 | 68,800.39 | 31,199.61 |
| 19 | 877.58 | 826.20 | 51.38 | 99,093.18 | 67,374.04 | 32,625.96 |
| 20 | 877.58 | 825.78 | 51.80 | 99,041.38 | 65,975.79 | 34,024.21 |
| 21 | 877.58 | 825.34 | 52.24 | 98,989.14 | 64,605.08 | 35,394.92 |
| 22 | 877.58 | 824.91 | 52.67 | 98,936.47 | 63,261.36 | 36,738.64 |

**Table 10-2.** (Cont.)

| Month | Payment | Interest | Principal | Remaining Balance | 2% Prepay | Principal |
|---|---|---|---|---|---|---|
| 23 | 877.58 | 824.47 | 53.11 | 98,883.36 | 61,944.09 | 38,055.91 |
| 24 | 877.58 | 824.03 | 53.55 | 98,829.81 | 60,652.73 | 39,347.27 |
| 25 | 877.58 | 823.58 | 54.00 | 98,775.81 | 59,386.75 | 40,613.25 |
| 26 | 877.58 | 823.13 | 54.45 | 98,721.36 | 58,145.66 | 41,854.34 |
| 27 | 877.58 | 822.68 | 54.90 | 98,666.46 | 56,928.94 | 43,071.06 |
| 28 | 877.58 | 822.22 | 55.36 | 98,611.10 | 55,736.11 | 44,263.89 |
| 29 | 877.58 | 821.76 | 55.82 | 98,555.28 | 54,566.68 | 45,433.32 |
| 30 | 877.58 | 821.29 | 56.29 | 98,498.99 | 53,420.19 | 46,579.81 |
| 31 | 877.58 | 820.82 | 56.76 | 98,442.24 | 52,296.17 | 47,703.83 |
| 32 | 877.58 | 820.35 | 57.23 | 98,385.01 | 51,194.16 | 48,805.84 |
| 33 | 877.58 | 819.88 | 57.70 | 98,327.31 | 50,113.73 | 49,886.27 |
| 34 | 877.58 | 819.39 | 58.19 | 98,269.12 | 49,054.43 | 50,945.57 |
| 35 | 877.58 | 818.91 | 58.67 | 98,210.45 | 48,015.84 | 51,984.16 |
| 36 | 877.58 | 818.42 | 59.16 | 98,151.29 | 46,997.55 | 53,002.45 |
| 37 | 877.58 | 817.93 | 59.65 | 98,091.64 | 45,999.14 | 54,000.86 |
| 38 | 877.58 | 817.43 | 60.15 | 98,031.49 | 45,020.21 | 54,979.79 |
| 39 | 877.58 | 816.93 | 60.65 | 97,970.84 | 44,060.37 | 55,939.63 |
| 40 | 877.58 | 816.42 | 61.16 | 97,909.68 | 43,119.23 | 56,880.77 |
| 41 | 877.58 | 815.91 | 61.67 | 97,848.01 | 42,196.41 | 57,803.59 |
| 42 | 877.58 | 815.40 | 62.18 | 97,785.83 | 41,291.55 | 58,708.45 |
| 43 | 877.58 | 814.88 | 62.70 | 97,723.14 | 40,404.27 | 59,595.73 |
| 44 | 877.58 | 814.36 | 63.22 | 97,659.92 | 39,534.23 | 60,465.77 |

**Table 10-2. (Cont.)**

| Month | Payment | Interest | Principal | Remaining Balance | 2% Prepay | Principal |
|---|---|---|---|---|---|---|
| 45 | 877.58 | 813.83 | 63.75 | 97,596.17 | 38,681.07 | 61,318.93 |
| 46 | 877.58 | 813.30 | 64.28 | 97,531.89 | 37,844.46 | 62,155.54 |
| 47 | 877.58 | 812.77 | 64.81 | 97,467.07 | 37,024.05 | 62,975.95 |
| 48 | 877.58 | 812.23 | 65.35 | 97,401.72 | 36,219.52 | 63,780.48 |
| 49 | 877.58 | 811.68 | 65.90 | 97,335.82 | 35,430.55 | 64,569.45 |
| 50 | 877.58 | 811.13 | 66.45 | 97,269.37 | 34,656.82 | 65,343.18 |
| 51 | 877.58 | 810.58 | 67.00 | 97,202.37 | 33,898.02 | 66,101.98 |
| 52 | 877.58 | 810.02 | 67.56 | 97,134.81 | 33,153.85 | 66,846.15 |
| 53 | 877.58 | 809.46 | 68.12 | 97,066.69 | 32,424.01 | 67,575.99 |
| 54 | 877.58 | 808.89 | 68.69 | 96,998.00 | 31,708.22 | 68,291.78 |
| 55 | 877.58 | 808.32 | 69.26 | 96,928.73 | 31,006.18 | 68,993.82 |
| 56 | 877.58 | 807.74 | 69.84 | 96,858.89 | 30,317.61 | 69,682.39 |
| 57 | 877.58 | 807.16 | 70.42 | 96,788.47 | 29,642.24 | 70,357.76 |
| 58 | 877.58 | 806.57 | 71.01 | 96,717.46 | 28,979.81 | 71,020.19 |
| 59 | 877.58 | 805.98 | 71.60 | 96,645.86 | 28,330.04 | 71,669.96 |
| 60 | 877.58 | 805.38 | 72.20 | 96,573.66 | 27,692.69 | 72,307.31 |
| 61 | 877.58 | 804.78 | 72.80 | 96,500.86 | 27,067.49 | 72,932.51 |
| 62 | 877.58 | 804.17 | 73.41 | 96,427.46 | 26,454.20 | 73,545.80 |
| 63 | 877.58 | 803.56 | 74.02 | 96,353.44 | 25,852.58 | 74,147.42 |
| 64 | 877.58 | 802.95 | 74.63 | 96,278.80 | 25,262.39 | 74,737.61 |
| 65 | 877.58 | 802.32 | 75.26 | 96,203.55 | 24,683.39 | 75,316.61 |

**Table 10-2.** (Cont.)

| Month | Payment | Interest | Principal | Remaining Balance | 2% Prepay | Principal |
|---|---|---|---|---|---|---|
| 66 | 877.58 | 801.70 | 75.88 | 96,127.66 | 24,115.35 | 75,884.65 |
| 67 | 877.58 | 801.06 | 76.52 | 96,051.15 | 23,558.06 | 76,441.94 |
| 68 | 877.58 | 800.43 | 77.15 | 95,973.99 | 23,011.29 | 76,988.71 |
| 69 | 877.58 | 799.78 | 77.80 | 95,896.20 | 22,474.82 | 77,525.18 |
| 70 | 877.58 | 799.13 | 78.45 | 95,817.75 | 21,948.45 | 78,051.55 |
| 71 | 877.58 | 798.48 | 79.10 | 95,738.65 | 21,431.96 | 78,568.04 |
| 72 | 877.58 | 797.82 | 79.76 | 95,658.90 | 20,925.16 | 79,074.84 |
| 73 | 877.58 | 797.16 | 80.42 | 95,578.47 | 20,427.85 | 79,572.15 |
| 74 | 877.58 | 796.49 | 81.09 | 95,497.38 | 19,939.82 | 80,060.18 |
| 75 | 877.58 | 795.81 | 81.77 | 95,415.61 | 19,460.89 | 80,539.11 |
| 76 | 877.58 | 795.13 | 82.45 | 95,333.16 | 18,990.87 | 81,009.13 |
| 77 | 877.58 | 794.44 | 83.14 | 95,250.02 | 18,529.58 | 81,470.42 |
| 78 | 877.58 | 793.75 | 83.83 | 95,166.19 | 18,076.83 | 81,923.17 |
| 79 | 877.58 | 793.05 | 84.53 | 95,081.67 | 17,632.46 | 82,367.54 |
| 80 | 877.58 | 792.35 | 85.23 | 94,996.43 | 17,196.28 | 82,803.72 |
| 81 | 877.58 | 791.64 | 85.94 | 94,910.49 | 16,768.13 | 83,231.87 |
| 82 | 877.58 | 790.92 | 86.66 | 94,823.83 | 16,347.84 | 83,652.16 |
| 83 | 877.58 | 790.20 | 87.38 | 94,736.45 | 15,935.25 | 84,064.75 |
| 84 | 877.58 | 789.47 | 88.11 | 94,648.34 | 15,530.20 | 84,469.80 |
| 85 | 877.58 | 788.74 | 88.84 | 94,559.50 | 15,132.53 | 84,867.47 |
| 86 | 877.58 | 788.00 | 89.58 | 94,469.91 | 14,742.09 | 85,257.91 |
| 87 | 877.58 | 787.25 | 90.33 | 94,379.58 | 14,358.72 | 85,641.28 |

**Table 10-2. (Cont.)**

| Month | Payment | Interest | Principal | Remaining Balance | 2% Prepay | Principal |
|-------|---------|----------|-----------|-------------------|-----------|-----------|
| 88 | 877.58 | 786.50 | 91.08 | 94,288.50 | 13,982.28 | 86,017.72 |
| 89 | 877.58 | 785.74 | 91.84 | 94,196.66 | 13,612.63 | 86,387.37 |
| 90 | 877.58 | 784.97 | 92.61 | 94,104.05 | 13,249.62 | 86,750.38 |
| 91 | 877.58 | 784.20 | 93.38 | 94,010.67 | 12,893.12 | 87,106.88 |
| 92 | 877.58 | 783.42 | 94.16 | 93,916.51 | 12,542.98 | 87,457.02 |
| 93 | 877.58 | 782.64 | 94.94 | 93,821.57 | 12,199.08 | 87,800.92 |
| 94 | 877.58 | 781.85 | 95.73 | 93,725.83 | 11,861.28 | 88,138.72 |
| 95 | 877.58 | 781.05 | 96.53 | 93,629.30 | 11,529.45 | 88,470.55 |
| 96 | 877.58 | 780.24 | 97.34 | 93,531.97 | 11,203.47 | 88,796.53 |
| 97 | 877.58 | 779.43 | 98.15 | 93,433.82 | 10,883.22 | 89,116.78 |
| 98 | 877.58 | 778.62 | 98.96 | 93,334.86 | 10,568.57 | 89,431.43 |
| 99 | 877.58 | 777.79 | 99.79 | 93,235.07 | 10,259.41 | 89,740.59 |
| 100 | 877.58 | 776.96 | 100.62 | 93,134.44 | 9,955.61 | 90,044.39 |
| 101 | 877.58 | 776.12 | 101.46 | 93,032.99 | 9,657.07 | 90,342.93 |
| 102 | 877.58 | 775.27 | 102.31 | 92,930.68 | 9,363.67 | 90,636.33 |
| 103 | 877.58 | 774.42 | 103.16 | 92,827.52 | 9,075.30 | 90,924.70 |
| 104 | 877.58 | 773.56 | 104.02 | 92,723.51 | 8,791.86 | 91,208.14 |
| 105 | 877.58 | 772.70 | 104.88 | 92,618.62 | 8,513.23 | 91,486.77 |
| 106 | 877.58 | 771.82 | 105.76 | 92,512.86 | 8,239.32 | 91,760.68 |
| 107 | 877.58 | 770.94 | 106.64 | 92,406.22 | 7,970.03 | 92,029.97 |
| 108 | 877.58 | 770.05 | 107.53 | 92,298.70 | 7,705.25 | 92,294.75 |
| 109 | 877.58 | 769.16 | 108.42 | 92,190.27 | 7,444.89 | 92,555.11 |

*Table 10-2. (Cont.)*

| Month | Payment | Interest | Principal | Remaining Balance | 2% Prepay | Principal |
|-------|---------|----------|-----------|-------------------|-----------|-----------|
| 110 | 877.58 | 768.25 | 109.33 | 92,080.94 | 7,188.85 | 92,811.15 |
| 111 | 877.58 | 767.34 | 110.24 | 91,970.70 | 6,937.04 | 93,062.96 |
| 112 | 877.58 | 766.42 | 111.16 | 91,859.55 | 6,689.37 | 93,310.63 |
| 113 | 877.58 | 765.50 | 112.08 | 91,747.46 | 6,445.74 | 93,554.26 |
| 114 | 877.58 | 764.56 | 113.02 | 91,634.45 | 6,206.06 | 93,793.94 |
| 115 | 877.58 | 763.62 | 113.96 | 91,520.49 | 5,970.26 | 94,029.74 |
| 116 | 877.58 | 762.67 | 114.91 | 91,405.58 | 5,738.25 | 94,261.75 |
| 117 | 877.58 | 761.71 | 115.87 | 91,289.71 | 5,509.93 | 94,490.07 |
| 118 | 877.58 | 760.75 | 116.83 | 91,172.88 | 5,285.24 | 94,714.76 |
| 119 | 877.58 | 759.77 | 117.81 | 91,055.07 | 5,064.08 | 94,935.92 |
| 120 | 877.58 | 758.79 | 118.79 | 90,936.28 | 4,846.39 | 95,153.61 |
| 121 | 877.58 | 757.80 | 119.78 | 90,816.51 | 4,632.08 | 95,367.92 |
| 122 | 877.58 | 756.80 | 120.78 | 90,695.73 | 4,421.08 | 95,578.92 |
| 123 | 877.58 | 755.80 | 121.78 | 90,573.95 | 4,213.31 | 95,786.69 |
| 124 | 877.58 | 754.78 | 122.80 | 90,451.15 | 4,008.70 | 95,991.30 |
| 125 | 877.58 | 753.76 | 123.82 | 90,327.33 | 3,807.18 | 96,192.82 |
| 126 | 877.58 | 752.73 | 124.85 | 90,202.48 | 3,608.69 | 96,391.31 |
| 127 | 877.58 | 751.69 | 125.89 | 90,076.59 | 3,413.14 | 96,586.86 |
| 128 | 877.58 | 750.64 | 126.94 | 89,949.64 | 3,220.47 | 96,779.53 |
| 129 | 877.58 | 749.58 | 128.00 | 89,821.64 | 3,030.62 | 96,969.38 |
| 130 | 877.58 | 748.51 | 129.07 | 89,692.58 | 2,843.52 | 97,156.48 |
| 131 | 877.58 | 747.44 | 130.14 | 89,562.44 | 2,659.12 | 97,340.88 |

**Table 10-2.** (Cont.)

| Month | Payment | Interest | Principal | Remaining Balance | 2% Prepay | Principal |
|---|---|---|---|---|---|---|
| 132 | 877.58 | 746.35 | 131.23 | 89,431.21 | 2,477.33 | 97,522.67 |
| 133 | 877.58 | 745.26 | 132.32 | 89,298.89 | 2,298.11 | 97,701.89 |
| 134 | 877.58 | 744.16 | 133.42 | 89,165.47 | 2,121.39 | 97,878.61 |
| 135 | 877.58 | 743.05 | 134.53 | 89,030.93 | 1,947.12 | 98,052.88 |
| 136 | 877.58 | 741.92 | 135.66 | 88,895.28 | 1,775.24 | 98,224.76 |
| 137 | 877.58 | 740.79 | 136.79 | 88,758.49 | 1,605.68 | 98,394.32 |
| 138 | 877.58 | 739.65 | 137.93 | 88,620.57 | 1,438.40 | 98,561.60 |
| 139 | 877.58 | 738.50 | 139.08 | 88,481.49 | 1,273.34 | 98,726.66 |
| 140 | 877.58 | 737.35 | 140.23 | 88,341.26 | 1,110.44 | 98,889.56 |
| 141 | 877.58 | 736.18 | 141.40 | 88,199.85 | 949.66 | 99,050.34 |
| 142 | 877.58 | 735.00 | 142.58 | 88,057.27 | 790.94 | 99,209.06 |
| 143 | 877.58 | 733.81 | 143.77 | 87,913.50 | 634.22 | 99,365.78 |
| 144 | 877.58 | 732.61 | 144.97 | 87,768.53 | 479.47 | 99,520.53 |
| 145 | 877.58 | 731.40 | 146.18 | 87,622.36 | 326.63 | 99,673.37 |
| 146 | 877.58 | 730.19 | 147.39 | 87,474.97 | 175.65 | 99,824.35 |
| 147 | 877.58 | 728.96 | 148.62 | 87,326.34 | 26.49 | 99,973.51 |
| 148 | 877.58 | 727.72 | 149.86 | 87,176.48 | -120.90 | 0 |

Let's go back to our five classes of bonds, each with a $20,000 face amount but with the following yields and average maturities:

Class A: yielding  8.0%—to be fully paid off in 3 years
Class B: yielding  8.5%—to be fully paid off in 6 years
Class C: yielding  9.0%—to be fully paid off in 12 years
Class D: yielding  9.5%—to be fully paid off in 20 years
Class E: yielding 10.0%—to be fully paid off in 30 years

When the effects of prepayments are taken into account, the Class A bonds would be retired as follows:

11 bonds at the 6-month point
 9 bonds at the 12-month point

Class B bonds would be retired as follows:

2 bonds at the 12-month point
9 bonds at the 18-month point
8 bonds at the 24-month point
1 bond at the 30-month point

Class C bonds would be retired as follows:

6 bonds at the 30-month point
7 bonds at the 36-month point
5 bonds at the 42-month point
2 bonds at the 48-month point

Class D bonds would be retired as follows:

3 bonds at the 48-month point
5 bonds at the 54-month point
4 bonds at the 60-month point
3 bonds at the 66-month point
4 bonds at the 72-month point
1 bond at the 78-month point

Class E bonds would be retired as follows:

1 bond at the 78-month point
3 bonds at the 84-month point
2 bonds at the 90-month point
2 bonds at the 96-month point
2 bonds at the 102-month point
2 bonds at the 108-month point
1 bonds at the 114-month point
2 bonds at the 120-month point
1 bond at the 126-month point
1 bond at the 132-month point
1 bond at the 138-month point
1 bond at the 144-month point
1 bond at the 150-month point

Thus the average life of the different classes is

Class A: $(66 + 108) / 20 = 8.7$ months
Class B: $(24 + 162 + 192 + 30) / 20 = 20.4$ months
Class C: $(180 + 252 + 210 + 96) / 20 = 36.9$ months
Class D: $(144 + 240 + 240 + 198 + 288 + 78) / 20 = 59.4$ months
Class E: $(78 + 252 + 180 + 192 + 204 + 216 + 114 + 240 + 126 +$
$\quad 132 + 138 + 144 + 150) / 20 = 108.3$ months

As you can see, prepayments dramatically shorten the maturity of all the classes.

Class A: 8.0%—from 36 months to 8.7 months
Class B: 8.5%—from 72 months to 20.4 months
Class C: 9.0%—from 144 months to 36.9 months
Class D: 9.5%—from 240 months to 59.4 months
Class E: 10.0%—from 360 months to 108.3 months

Assuming an 8% reinvestment rate, the RCY of the above bonds would be

Class A: 8.000%
Class B: 8.453%
Class C: 8.855%
Class D: 9.220%
Class E: 9.321%

Of course, if we assume a 12% reinvestment rate, then the bonds would offer realized compound yields of:

Class A:  8.094%
Class B:  8.750%
Class C:  9.431%
Class D:  9.972%
Class E: 10.720%

There have recently been a whole host of new spin-off CMO structures created by the various intermediates to meet the specific investment needs of the different niches of the market. However, none of these have eliminated the analytical problems inherent in MBSs.

## Chapter 11

# Floating-Rate Bonds

A *floating-rate bond* is a bond that pays an interest rate that rises and falls in relation to an index rate. Thus when market interest rates go up, the index rate rises and so does the yield that the vehicle pays. The opposite happens when market interest rates fall.

Investors for whom floating-rate bonds are attractive are investors for whom the preserving principal is more important than earning a higher yield. Primarily, these investors fall into two classes:

1. those who want to match their assets with their liabilities (i.e., commercial banks)
2. those who want a substitute for money-market instruments.

For example, a large part of a commercial bank's lendable funds come from deposits, either demand deposits (savings and checking accounts) or short-term certificates of deposit. The rate of interest that the bank has to pay to attract these deposits determines, to a large de-

gree, the bank's cost of funds. The bank makes its profit by relend-
ing these funds at a higher interest rate (i.e., a positive yield spread).
However, as we covered in Chapter 10, the bank exposes itself to the
risk that if it makes a long-term fixed-rate loan and its cost of funds
increases, it may end up with a negative, instead of a positive, spread
on its loan portfolio.

If, instead of making fixed-rate loans, the bank makes floating-rate
loans, or *invests* in floating-rate bonds, it largely eliminates this
spread risk. Of course the bank still has to contend with credit risk. A
bank might also elect to *issue* floating-rate bonds and then loan the
proceeds of the bond issue at a higher floating rate, again locking in a
positive yield spread.

A second reason to invest in floating-rate notes is as a higher-
yielding alternative to money-market instruments. By investing in
floaters, the investor can earn a higher yield without being exposed to
the interest-rate risk that's usually associated with longer-term bonds.

## The Components of Fixed-Rate
## vs. Floating-Rate Vehicles

Before we discuss the specifics of these vehicles, it's worthwhile
to do a brief comparison of the three components that make up a
fixed-rate bond's TDR and a floating-rate-bond's TDR.

For both fixed-rate and floating-rate securities, you can predict the
principal component exactly—assuming you hold the bonds to maturity and all the principal and interest payments are made in full and on
time.

The interest component can be predicted exactly for fixed-rate
bonds but not for floating-rate bonds because the interest component
for floating-rate bonds is dependent upon future interest rates. Thus a
prediction of the TDR of a floater is always less accurate than a prediction of the TDR of a fixed-rate bond.

Of course, you will not be able to make an accurate prediction of
the IOI component for either type of bond.

## Selecting Floating-Rate Bonds

If you want to earn a competitive return without assuming interest-rate risk, you must be very careful when you select floating-rate instruments in which to invest. The factors you need to consider before purchasing a floating-rate instrument include

1. the index on which the security's yield is based
2. the yield spread between the index and the security
3. the issue's credit rating
4. the frequency with which the security's yield is adjusted
5. the frequency with which the security pays interest
6. the security's minimum and/or maximum yield—if any
7. the security's call and put provisions
8. the security's convertibility features.

Only when you know these eight factors can you evaluate a given floating-rate security accurately. Let's explore each of these factors in some detail.

### Index

The yields paid by dollar-denominated floating-rate securities are based on (or, in the vernacular of the Street, are "priced off of") a number of different indexes. The most commonly used indexes are the London money rate, the U.S. Treasury rates, and the composite index compiled by the Federal Reserve Bank of New York.

The London money rate, or the *LIBOR (London Interbank Offering Rate)*, is the one used most often. This is the rate at which major London banks lend each other Eurodollars. Closely related to LIBOR is *LIBID* (the bid rate for these same deposits and *LIMEAN* (the mean average of LIBOR and LIBID). The spread between LIBID and LIBOR is usually one eighth. Thus with LIBOR at 10¹/₈, LIBID would usually be 10 and LIMEAN would be 10$^1$/16. If you had three securities: one that yields 1 point over LIBOR, one that yields 1$^1$/8 over LIBID, and one that yields 1$^1$/16 over LIMEAN, under normal circumstances they would all pay the same interest rate.

The LIBOR quote used to fix the rate of a new offering is usually the quote available on Reuters News Service at 11:00 A.M. on the day of the offering. When the rate a floater pays is going to be reset, the LIBOR quote used is usually the 11:00 A.M. Reuters LIBOR quote from two days prior to the reset date.

Another commonly used index consists of the U.S. Treasury rates. Included in this index are the original-issue discount rate for 91-day Treasury bills, the secondary-market yield for 91-day Treasury bills, and the Treasury Constant Yields for 1-, 2-, 5-, 10-, and 20-year U.S. government bond yields. (The Treasury Constant Yield is determined by averaging the yields of all reported trades for a given maturity on a given day.) All of these index rates are published by the Federal Reserve Bank of New York.

Other Indexes include a given bank's prime rate, the federal funds rate, the AA commercial-paper rate, the average domestic certificate-of-deposit rate, and some other unusual indexes (including the price of west Texas crude oil).

Floating-rate vehicles denominated in foreign currencies, of course, have their own indexes, including LIBOR (currency-adjusted) and the value of the European currency unit.

The indexes are not equally attractive, and their relative attractiveness can change over time in response to a wide variety of fiscal, monetary, and political factors.

Consider the following example:

Assume that on January 1, 1987, the 91-day Treasury bill yields 9% and LIBOR is 10%. You have a choice between floating-rate bond A, which yields 2 points over the primary Treasury-bill rate, and floating-rate bond B, which yields 1 point over LIBOR. (The LIBOR rate is generally higher than the Treasury-bill rate, and so a floater must usually offer a wider spread over the Treasury-bill index in order to be competitive.) Assuming all other factors are the same, it would appear that the two securities offer the investor the same return, at least initially.

If, however, after making the investment, there was a shock to the international financial system or interest rates rose sharply, investors would, quite predictably and understandably, start a "flight to quality." In other words, they would move money out of the international banking system and into Treasury bills because Treasury bills have no credit risk. This would cause the spread between the Treasury-bill rate and the LIBOR rate to increase. Thus, if you selected the Treasury-bill-based floater, you would end up with a lower rate of return than if you selected the LIBOR-based floater.

On the other hand, if interest rates declined and investors in general had a lot of confidence in the international banking system, the yield spread between the Treasury-bill rate and the LIBOR rate might shrink. If this spread shrank and you had selected the Treasury-bill-based floater, you would have a better return. Thus, before you select your index, make some assumptions about which way interest rates are going to move and how likely it is that the international banking system will remain sound over the term of your investment. The Treasury-bill/LIBOR spread has been as low as 25 basis points and as high as 450 basis points.

Investors who believe that banks are quick to raise their prime rate when interest rates move up but are slow to lower their prime when interest rates move down may find the prime rate to be an attractive index. If you are right about the speed with which a bank raises and lowers its prime rate, then the bank will be quick to raise the yield your floating-rate bonds pay when interest rates rise and slow to lower your bonds' yield when interest rates fall.

Floaters pegged to the prime rate have a *negative spread*. In other words, they usually yield less than prime because the prime rate is usually higher than the Treasury-bill rate or the LIBOR rate. Thus, the selection of which index your floating-rate investment is pegged to can have a dramatic effect on your overall return. The LIBOR/prime rate spread has been as low as minus 200 basis points and as high as plus 475 basis points.

## Yield Spread

The spread between the floater and the index is determined primarily by the credit quality of the issuer. Many of the issuers of floaters have an investment-grade rating. Again, your outlook for future interest rates is a factor in determining the relative attractiveness of different floating-rate bonds with different credit ratings.

Consider the following example:

Assume you have a choice between an AAA-rated floater pegged at 1 point over LIBOR and an A-rated floater pegged at 2 points over LIBOR when LIBOR is at 8%. Your choice is thus between an AAA security yielding 9% or an A-rated security yielding 10%. You compute the difference in return on a percentage basis and find that you could earn 11.11% more by investing in the lower-priced security. You feel this extra yield is a fair extra return for assuming the extra credit risk of the lower-priced security. It would appear that on a risk/reward basis, the two securities are equally attractive, and so you flip a coin and end up buying the higher-rated security.

If interest rates decline to a point where LIBOR is yielding 4%, the two securities will be yielding 5% and 6%, respectively. At these yields, the lower-rated security offers a 20% higher return than the higher-rated security. Since you felt that 11.11% was a fair extra return for the extra credit risk, if interest rates drop, the lower-rated security becomes relatively more attractive. Similarly, if interest rates rise, the same reasoning would make the higher-rated security a better buy. Therefore, selecting the best floater requires that you make some assumptions about the future direction and magnitude of interest-rate swings.

## Credit Rating

Once an issue's spread over its index has been established and the issue is sold, the spread that the issuer pays investors remains constant. This means that if an issue's credit rating changes, in order for the market to reflect the change, it has to adjust the bond's market price.

For example, when an AA-rated security is first offered, investors may accept a 1-point spread over LIBOR. If, however, after the security is issued, it is downgraded from AA to BBB, investors might want a spread of 3 points over LIBOR. Since the interest rate the issuer pays is fixed at 1 point over LIBOR, the market will drop the issue's price until its yield is equal to approximately LIBOR plus 3. Thus even the market value of a floating-rate bond is susceptible to credit risk.

## Frequency of Adjustment

The interest rate that some floaters pay is adjusted weekly, while the interest rate others pay is adjusted only every few years. Some generalizations can be made about the frequency at which interest rates are adjusted.

First, all other factors being identical, the more frequently a security adjusts its interest rate the less its principal value will fluctuate. This is true because a security that adjusts its interest rates more frequently will yield a rate that is always closer to the current market rate.

Consider the following example:

Assume you have a choice between a floating-rate security that adjusts its return on a weekly basis and one that adjusts its return on a biannual basis. All other factors, including yield, are equal. If you select the security with the longer adjustment period and interest rates rise, you lose. This is because while the other security is yielding more every week as interest rates rise, your security is yielding a lower rate, which becomes progressively less competitive. Adding insult to injury, if you sell your bond, you will have to price it so that the overall return to the next adjustment date is competitive (i.e., sell it at a discount).

On the other hand, if interest rates decline, you will be better off because your infrequently adjusting security will yield an above-market return until the next adjustment date, while the weekly floater will earn progressively less with each weekly yield adjustment.

From this example, we can make a second generalization. When you expect interest rates to rise, invest in floaters with short (weekly or monthly) readjustment periods. If you expect interest rates to decline, you want the longest readjustment period that's consistent with your investment objectives and your tolerance for risk. As your expectations for interest rates change, you should also consider changing (swapping) the floating-rate securities in your portfolio for more appropriate issues.

## Frequency of Interest

Like any income-bearing security, the more frequently your security pays interest, the greater your potential for compounding interest. Thus, all other factors being equal, the greater the number of interest payments per year, the more attractive your bond becomes. A bond that offers a lower yield but makes frequent (daily or weekly) interest payments may be more attractive than a higher-yielding security that makes less-frequent interest payments (semiannually or weekly). The reason for this is that the first bond provides more opportunity to accumulate IOI.

## Minimum and/or Maximum Yield

Many floaters have minimum and maximum yields that they can pay. These are specified in the offering memorandum. Maximum yields protect the issuer, while minimum yields protect the investor. As a security approaches its minimum or maximum, it begins to act less like a floating-rate security and more like a fixed-rate security with a coupon yield equal to maximum yield.

Consider the following example:

Assume that a 10-year floating-rate security is pegged at 2 points over the 91-day Treasury-bill rate and has a maximum yield of 13%. As long as the Treasury-bill rate stays at or below 11%, the security will offer a competitive return. However, if the Treasury-bill rate rises higher than 11%, the floater will no longer be able to adjust its interest rate and thus will become progressively less competitive if interest rates continue to rise. The higher the Treasury-bill rate rises, the less attractive the security's maximum yield of 13% becomes.

If, when the security has three years left until its final maturity date, the security matures in three years and the Treasury-bill rate is 18%, the floating-rate security would be priced at approximately $850. At this price, the security offers a yield to maturity of 20%. Note, however, that the security might sell for less than this price because once a floater reaches its bracket, a fixed-rate security that offers the same yield is more attractive.

The reason for this is that while both bonds offer the same maximum return if held to maturity, the floater could offer a lower return if interest rates dropped sharply over the 3-year period. While the fixed-rate bond would always offer the higher yield, the floater's yield could drop, resulting in a lower return to the investor.

Minimum yields have the opposite effect. Once a floating security is yielding its minimum allowable coupon, any further decline in the security's index rate will cause the floater to offer a yield that is more than competitive, and the market will adjust the price of the security upwards. In fact, in the opinion of this author, one of the best times to buy floating-rate securities is when they are close to yielding their minimum allowable yields.

Once purchased, if index rates decline, you get an above-market return and the potential for price appreciation. If interest rates rise, you get a progressively higher return with principal preservation. Also, since the security is near its minimum yield, interest rates would have to shoot up substantially before the security would approach its maximum yield. Thus you have a win-win situation when you buy a floater near its minimum yield.

## Call and Put Provisions

Floaters also frequently come with call and put provisions. *Call provisions* allow the issuer to retire the securities (at par or slightly over par) before their scheduled maturity. An issuer would call an issue when the funds were no longer needed or when the funds were available from another source at a lower net financing cost. Calls usually work to the detriment of the investor.

*Put provisions* allow the investor to return the security to the issuer (usually at par) before the security's scheduled maturity. You would exercise this option if you needed the funds you invested in the security for another purpose or if you found a more attractive investment opportunity. Put provisions generally work to the advantage of the investor because they allow him to bail out of an investment that is no longer attractive without having to take a market loss.

Consider the following two examples:

1. A floating-rate security is issued with its interest rate pegged at 1 1/2 points over LIBOR. A few years later, new issues of similar securities with similar credit ratings are being successfully offered at LIBOR-plus-one-half. In this case, the issuer is overpaying by 1 point per year and may elect to call this particular issue and put out another issue of floaters at the now marketable rate of 1/2 point over LIBOR. In this case, the call feature was very attractive to the issuer.

   On the other hand, if the spread over LIBOR widened over time, the investors would have exercised their puts and would have then had their funds free to reinvest at the then wider spread.

2. You invest in an A-rated security that is pegged to yield 2 1/2 points over Treasury bills. After you buy the security, it is downgraded to a BBB-rated security. The spread is fixed, so the market has little choice but to lower the security's price. In this event, having a put feature is very attractive to the investor.

   On the other hand, if the security's credit rating improves, having a call privilege is very beneficial to the issuer.

Investors should make certain that the put provisions are at least as generous as the call provisions. A security that allows the issuer to call it on an annual basis but allows you to put it back to the issuer only every five years is not as attractive as is a *symmetrical bond* (one with equal put and call provisions).

Generally, investors who buy floaters are seeking a market return with a minimum of risk and are not out to make a killing. These investors are not bothered by having a security with call provisions. After all, if they really felt strongly that interest rates were going to decline to the point where the floater would reach its lower bracket and appreciate, they would buy fixed-rate or zero-coupon debt.

## Convertible Features

Floating-rate securities may have conversion features that will dramatically affect their value. This conversion feature can give either the investor or the issuer the option of converting the floating-rate bond into another type of security, usually either fixed-rate debt or common stock. Some floating-rate securities also allow the investor to change the type of index the security is based upon. Since convertible bonds are covered in another chapter, we'll restrict ourselves to discussing conversion into fixed-rate debt and changing indexes in this section.

Having a floating-rate issue that is convertible into fixed-rate debt can be very beneficial to the issuer, but it is usually *not* beneficial to the investor.

Consider the following example:

Assume that on January 2, 1987, a company wants to borrow $100,000,000 for 20 years in order to finance an acquisition. The company prefers to borrow at a fixed rate so that it will know what its future costs will be and thus can do its planning with some degree of certainty. Unfortunately for the company, its investment bankers tell it that the best rate it can expect to get on a 20-year bond offering is 15%. At a 15% financing cost, the acquisition is barely profitable, and so the company decides to walk away from the acquisition.

But then another (smarter) investment banking firm suggests that the company issue a floating-rate bond that is

callable in the fifth year and each year thereafter

putable in the fifth year and each year thereafter

convertible into fixed-rate debt

has a minimum yield of 7% and a maximum yield of 13%

is pegged at $1^{1}/2$% over the 1-year treasury constant

pays interest on a semiannual basis.

Since the investor looking at this bond can put it back to the issuer in five years at par, and since the bond's interest rate is adjusted every year (within the 7%–13% parameter), investors are very attracted to this bond even though it may only yield 9% (assuming the 1-year treasury constant rate is 7½%).

Thus:

1. The company is able to borrow at a lower cost (9% vs. 15%) than it could with a fixed-rate instrument.
2. The company knows that for the first five years, its financing costs will not exceed 13% regardless of what happens to interest rates. At a financing cost of 13%, the acquisition can be successful—although not hugely profitable.
3. The company has the potential for lower financing costs if interest rates decline.

On the other hand, there are some disadvantages to this type of financing.

1. The company does not know what its overall financing cost will be, making planning very difficult.
2. The company cannot count on having the money for 20 years because the entire issue might be put back to it in 5 years' time.

To partially solve these last two problems, the company might attach a *drop-lock provision* to its floating-rate bonds. This provision would state that if interest rates for fixed-rate debt with a similar maturity and credit rating got to a certain level, the floating-rate bonds would convert into fixed-rate bonds with a predetermined coupon.

It might, for example, state that "should the Shearson Lehman bond index yield 9% or less for three consecutive days, the issue at its next interest payment date will become a fixed-rate bond yielding 10% until its scheduled maturity." This means that if the Shearson Lehman bond index drops to 9% at the end of the third year, the floater will become a 17-year, 10% fixed-rate bond on the next interest payment date. If you want fixed-rate paper, you can keep it; if not, since the rate that your bond pays is slightly higher than the index (or market) rate, you should be able to sell it for par (or slightly over par) unless its credit-worthiness has declined. You can then reinvest your funds in another floating-rate security.

By forcing conversion, the issuer gets the long-term fixed-rate money it originally wanted, except at a lower cost (10% vs. 15%). As an investor, you are able to buy the issuer's 20-year bond without assuming the interest-rate risk that's inherent in 20-year fixed-rate paper. Again, a win-win situation.

The second type of convertibility feature is one that allows you as the investor to select which index you want to use. For example, a floater might give you a choice of 1% over LIBOR or 2% over Treasury bills. You would select whichever index formula gives you the highest yield. Initially, it might be the Treasury-based formula; but if interest rates rise or there is a shock to the banking system, the LIBOR rate may be more attractive.

Issuers give you this flexibility to make their issues more attractive. Since these issues are more attractive to investors, they generally offer a lower spread over the indexes than do nonconvertible issues.

## Determining Yields and Analyzing Floaters

The formulas for computing the coupon, nominal, and current yields for fixed- and floating-rate securities are the same. However, the formulas for computing yield to maturity are different. With a fixed-rate security, you have all the variables you need to compute a precise YTM except the reinvestment rate that you assume. With a floater, however, there are two unknowns: (1) the reinvestment rate and (2) the reinvestment amount. These variables are such a large portion of the formula that if you have to use assumptions for both of these factors, the results you get from the formula are practically meaningless. Although there are numerous software packages and analysis methods available, they all require that you make these assumptions, and so their real-world utility is questionable.

Instead, evaluating floaters is, for all practical purposes, limited to doing a comparative rather than an absolute analysis. If your objectives are such that floaters are a suitable investment vehicle, you can compare the various floating-rate issues against the universe of similar issues with respect to the variables detailed above.

For the most part, the floating market is a very liquid one, suitable to short-term trading. Issues pegged to LIBOR generally trade in 5MM dollar pieces (with 1MM-pieces representing good delivery). Issues pegged to Treasury bills generally trade in 1MM pieces (with 100K being good delivery).

Floating-rate securities are also very suitable to bondswaps.

# Chapter 12

# *Bondswaps*

A *bondswap* is selling one bond and replacing it with another that you find more attractive. Since your objectives and your expectations about future interest rates, credit quality, and so on will change over time, the best bonds for your portfolio will also change over time. Further, you may decide that a certain bond is either underpriced or overpriced in the marketplace. If you're right, then selling the overpriced issue and buying the underpriced issue will increase your portfolio's return. Let's examine, in some detail, the different reasons for swapping bonds.

## Rate-Anticipation Swap

The most common reason for swapping bonds is that you expect market interest rates to rise when they have been declining or to decline when they have been rising.

When you expect market interest rates to *decline,* you want your bond portfolio to be composed of long-term, fixed-rate, low-coupon (or zero-coupon) bonds. When you buy these bonds, you lock in a high current return and create a portfolio that will experience significant capital appreciation as interest rates decline. Bonds fitting this description have a long duration.

When you expect market interest rates to *increase,* you want your portfolio to consist of either (1) floating-rate bonds pegged to the best index or (2) short-term, fixed-rate, high-coupon bonds so that your portfolio will be protected from large capital losses as interest rates increase. Naturally, these bonds have short durations. This type of swap is commonly referred to as a *rate-anticipation swap.*

When you expect interest rates to rise and therefore shorten the weighted maturity of your portfolio, you also usually accept a lower current return in exchange for assuming less interest-rate risk. You need to examine the loss of this current income relative to the magnitude of the anticipated capital loss when you are evaluating a rate-anticipation swap.

For example, if the result of a given swap is that you eliminate a *probable* 30% principal loss in exchange for a 2% loss of current income, the swap makes sense. However, if the swap requires that you sacrifice 5% a year of current income in exchange for eliminating the probability of a 5% principal loss, the swap does *not* make sense.

## Substitution Swap

Another type of swap that is commonly available is a substitution swap. In a *substitution swap*, you replace a bond in your portfolio with a bond that is substantially identical (for example, you swap one "A"-rated, 20-year utility bond for another A-rated, 20-year utility bond) but, because of a temporary supply/demand discrepancy, is selling for a lower price (and thus a higher yield). By selling the bond you own and replacing it with the second bond, you increase your portfolio's return.

The supply/demand imbalances that make for profitable substitution swaps do not last very long because the market tends to be quickly self-correcting. Therefore it's important to be prepared to move very quickly when these situations arise.

## Credit Swap

Another type of swap that you should be open to and looking for is a *credit swap*. In this type of swap, you sell a bond whose credit rating is deteriorating and try to replace it with a bond whose credit strength is improving. If you are successful, you replace an asset that will decline in value with one that will increase in value.

To obtain information about a given bond's credit strength, you should review the credit watch lists published by the major rating agencies and consider subscribing to one or more of the newsletters that try to anticipate changes in the credit ratings of different issues. Your broker may also have access to in-house bond-research departments that can provide you with bond credit information. While this type of swap is always appropriate, it's especially important to "firm up" the credit strength of your bond portfolio prior to a period of sharply rising market interest rates or severe economic downturns. The reason for this is that higher market interest rates and economic recessions will cause an increase in the number of bond issues that have their credit ratings downgraded or go into default. Of course, if you own any "junk bonds," continuous monitoring of the credit quality of your holdings is absolutely mandatory.

## Sector Swap

Another type of swap is called the *sector swap*. Sector swaps provide you with another way to incrementally increase the return from your portfolio. Some sectors of the bond market are, at any given time, more or less attractive (on a relative risk-adjusted basis) than other sectors of the bond market. For example, at different times, U.S. government securities may be more or less attractive than Ginnie Maes, which, in turn, may be more or less attractive than AAA-rated utility bonds, which may be more or less attractive than A-rated corporates, and so on.

Each sector of the bond market has a historic yield spread (expressed as a percentage) with every other sector of the bond market. However, different sectors of the market are sometimes overpriced or underpriced relative to the other sectors for reasons that have little to do with the relative value of the bonds.

Temporary surges in supply and demand, temporary increases or decreases in the popularity of a specific sector, and so on can distort the historic sector yield spreads. For example, the price of oil company bonds often rises and falls in concert with the price of oil, even for the strongest of oil companies. By buying low and selling high, you can incrementally increase the return of your portfolio.

Your broker or your trading desk can provide you up-to-the-minute information about which sectors "look cheap" at any one point in time. As the spread between the different sectors returns to normal, you may experience reasonably consistent small capital gains on your portfolio.

## Tax Swap

Still another type of swap is the *tax swap*. This is not the traditional type of tax swap, in which you sell bonds on which you have losses and replace them with similar bonds in order to accelerate your tax losses. Instead, this type of swap entails replacing taxable debt with tax-free debt and vice versa. Municipal bonds sometimes offer significantly higher after-tax returns that do taxable bonds, and sometimes they offer significantly *lower* after-tax returns.

As of the day this chapter is being written, tax-free bonds offer many investors significantly higher after-tax returns than do taxable bonds because a great deal of confusion surrounds the tax treatment of municipal securities. Some of the recent tax acts limit the exclusion of interest earned on specific types of municipal securities. Because the resulting confusion has caused many investors to shy away from all municipals, the yield of municipals has increased relative to the yield offered by taxable bonds.

If in the future, however, it appears that federal income taxes will be increased, investors will flock to municipals in anticipation of this increase and the after-tax yields of municipals will fall below the after-tax yields.

## Objectives Swap

Over time, your objectives may change. For example, when you are young, you may be interested in maximizing your returns, whereas as you approach retirement, your principal objective may be to generate a decent return without taking much credit risk. This change of objectives will usually necessitate your replacing your existing bond portfolio with a different portfolio.

Regardless of which type of swap you are considering, evaluate your existing portfolio against the universe of available replacement bonds. The advent of computerized data bases makes finding attractive swap candidates much easier than doing swaps "by hand." By establishing a set of quality, yield, and maturity screens, the computer can do most of the work for you and suggest a limited number of replacement alternatives for your consideration.

Given the increased volatility of interest rates, the proliferation of junk bonds, and the fragile state of our economy, every investor should consider using swaps as another tool in the fight to maximize returns and minimize risk.

# Chapter 13

# Portfolio Management

Basically, there are two ways to manage a bond portfolio: passively and actively. *Passive management* is the science or art of building a portfolio to meet a specific future liability schedule, to mirror the performance of the bond market as a whole, or to mirror the performance of a specific portion of the bond market. *Active management* is the science or art of trying to increase the yield of a given portfolio over what a comparable passive portfolio would yield by taking what the manager believes to be an acceptable amount of additional risk.

## Passive Management

Passive bond-portfolio managers do not try to outperform the market. They are satisfied with building a portfolio that has a very high probability of funding a specific future liability stream, performing as well as the market, or performing as well as a defined segment of the market. Let's consider these objectives.

## Funding Specific Liabilities

If a portfolio manager is fortunate enough to know with a high degree of certainty what his future liabilities will be, he can build a portfolio designed to fund this liability.

**Dedicated Portfolios.** The most obvious way to fund the future liability stream is to buy a series of U.S. government-backed zero-coupon bonds with maturities that correspond to the dates when future liabilities will be payable. By using this strategy, the investor eliminates reinvestment risk, credit risk, interest-rate risk, and the risk that the amount of dollars generated by the portfolio will be insufficient to meet the liability.

Consider the following example:

Assume that a company is obligated under its pension plan to pay a retired senior manager a pension of $100,000 a year for a period of 20 years, with the payments to be made on the first day of each year, beginning the first year after the employee retires. The simplest way to fund this liability would be with a matched portfolio of U.S. government zero-coupon bonds. Assuming a liquid market, if the yield curve for U.S. government zeros was shaped like Figure 8-3 on page 90, the company could build the bond portfolio today for a cost of $919,816.72 (see Table 13-1 opposite).

While this strategy will fund the company's future liability with a high degree of both certainty and simplicity, it is a very *expensive* solution to the problem because the average yield from a portfolio of U.S. government zero-coupon bonds is likely to be very low relative to other types of debt instruments available in the marketplace.

To make a dedicated portfolio less expensive, the portfolio manager might elect to use corporate zeros instead of government zeros. Because corporate zero-coupon bonds have a greater credit risk, they offer a higher yield.

Of course, by substituting corporate debt for government debt, the company is assuming some credit risk. This risk can be minimized in several ways.

First, the investor can make sure that his portfolio of corporate ZCBs is well diversified.

*Table 13-1.* The Cost of Building a Dedicated Portfolio to Fund a $100,000-a-Year Pension Liability for 20 Years with U.S. Government Zero-Coupon Bonds.

| Year | Liability | Discount Rate | Cost of Bonds |
|------|-----------|---------------|---------------|
| 1  | $ 100,000 | 5.7% | $ 94,607.38 |
| 2  | 100,000 | 6.1 | 88,831.96 |
| 3  | 100,000 | 7.0 | 81,629.79 |
| 4  | 100,000 | 7.6 | 74,602.08 |
| 5  | 100,000 | 8.0 | 68,058.32 |
| 6  | 100,000 | 8.2 | 62,321.29 |
| 7  | 100,000 | 8.4 | 56,858.45 |
| 8  | 100,000 | 8.6 | 51,684.63 |
| 9  | 100,000 | 8.9 | 46,424.70 |
| 10 | 100,000 | 9.0 | 42,241.08 |
| 11 | 100,000 | 9.1 | 38,364.34 |
| 12 | 100,000 | 9.2 | 34,779.90 |
| 13 | 100,000 | 9.3 | 31,472.98 |
| 14 | 100,000 | 9.4 | 28,428.73 |
| 15 | 100,000 | 9.5 | 25,632.34 |
| 16 | 100,000 | 9.6 | 23,069.13 |
| 17 | 100,000 | 9.7 | 20,724.65 |
| 18 | 100,000 | 9.8 | 18,584.80 |
| 19 | 100,000 | 9.9 | 16,635.81 |
| 20 | 100,000 | 10.0 | 14,864.36 |
|    | $2,000,000 |  | $919,816.72 |

Second, the investor can overfund the plan by a percentage equal to the anticipated default rate. For example, if the manager expects (due to either historical precedents or market analysis) that 1% of the bonds will default prior to maturity, the investor can overfund the liability by 1%. This reserve fund, which can be used to make up for any default, must be invested in short-term liquid vehicles. The difference between the yield of the reserve fund and the average yield of the portfolio will be a cost of using corporates.

Even including the cost of the *overfunding*, the corporate portfolio may still offer a higher return and thus lower cost.

**Annuities.** Another way to meet a future liability stream is to buy an annuity (or series of annuities) from an insurance company. If the investor purchases an annuity, the insurance company agrees to meet the future liability in exchange for a fixed cost today. The insurance company makes a profit if it is able to earn a higher return on the investor's dollars than it guarantees to pay the investor. The insurance company generally tries to earn a higher return by using one of the three strategies discussed below.

**Cash-Flow Matching.** *Cash-flow matching* is a relatively straightforward passive strategy that entails matching future cash flows from a bond portfolio with future liabilities. The last liability is the first to be matched, the next-to-last liability is the second to be matched, and so on, until all the liabilities are matched.

Going back to our pension-schedule example, the first liability that must be matched is the $100,000 liability that's due in 20 years.

If we assume that the yield curve for the type of bonds we want to use to build our portfolio resembles the one diagramed in Table 13-1, and that (for the sake of simplicity) we can purchase all the bonds we need at par, then the cost of funding the last liability will be $91,000. If we buy ninety-one 20-year, 10% bonds at par, then over the last year of the bond's life 20, it would generate the following cash flows:

$ 4,550 of interest at the 19$^1$/$_2$-year mark
$95,550 of principal and interest at the 20-year mark.

Assuming that the $4,550 is reinvested for six months at 5%, the $4,550 interest payment will yield an additional $112.50. Thus the total cash flow generated by these 91 bonds over the twentieth year is $100,212.50, enough to meet the $100,000 liability with a $212.50 surplus.

The next liability that must be matched is the $100,000 liability that's due at the end of the nineteenth year. In the nineteenth year, we are already receiving $4,550 at the 18$^1$/$_2$-year point and $4,550 at the 19-year point from the first bond we purchased. Again assuming that the earlier payment is reinvested for six months at 5% and yields

$122.50, the total liability at the 19-year point that's left for us to fund with a new bond purchase is

$$\$100,000 - \$4,550 - \$4,550 - \$112.50 = \$90,787.50$$

From the yield curve, we determine that 19-year bonds are yielding $9^3/4\%$. We then need to determine how many of these bonds we need to buy in order to fund our remaining liability of $90,787.50. If we buy 83 of the bonds, the cash flow from them in the nineteenth year will be

$ 4,046.25 at the $18^1/2$-year point
$86,046.25 at the 19-year point
$   101.16 IOI at the 19-year point from reinvesting the midyear coupon

The total received at the 19-year point will be $90,193.66, enough to fund our $90,787.50 liability with a $593.84 surplus.

Continuing this process for one more year, we find that for our $100,000 liability at the eighteenth year, we already have

$4,550 + $4,550 + $112.50 (from the 20-year bond)
  + $4,046.25 + $4,046.25 + $101.16 (from the 19-year bond)
  = $17,425.16 in cash flow from the first two bonds

Thus our remaining liability is $82,574.84.

Again from the yield curve, we determine that 18-year bonds are yielding $9^1/2\%$. Again we need to determine how many bonds we need to buy in order to fund our remaining liability. If we buy 76 of the bonds, the cash flow from them will be

$ 3,610.00 at the $17^1/2$-year point
$79,610.00 at the 18-year point
$    90.25 IOI from reinvesting the midyear coupon

The total received will be $83,310.25, enough to fund our $82,574.84 liability with a $735.41 surplus.

This process would then continue until the last liability was funded.

From this example, you can see that *the earlier the liability comes due, the greater the percentage of the liability that is funded by coupon payments of bonds that are used to meet later liabilities.* Because the bonds that are used to fund later liabilities are higher-yielding bonds, *the net effect of this strategy is that short-term liabilities are funded with long-term instruments without the concurrent reinvestment and interest-rate risk because there is little reinvestment and no sales of bonds prior to their maturity.*

Understand that the above example is, at best, a rough one. We assumed that we purchased all of the bonds used to meet the liabilities at par as a way of simplifying the calculations. In reality, this is seldom (if ever) the case, and, in fact, bonds that are selling at a premium are often the best bonds to use to fund a cash-flow matching portfolio (assuming they are noncallable). Also, the surplus that accumulates in the early years can often be used to reduce the number of bonds that need be bought to fund a later liability. Of course, buying fewer bonds to meet a later liability then also reduces cash flow in the early years which, in turn, reduces the surplus in later years.

If you think this is confusing, remember, too, that we have a very simple liability schedule. For a very complex liability schedule, the cash-flow calculating problems become infinitely more complex.

Therefore the best (and only practical way) to build a cash-flow matching portfolio is to use a relatively complex computer program to perform a mathematical technique called *linear optimization.* This technique develops the optimal portfolio from the universe of possible bond choices, *optimal portfolio* being defined as one that meets the liabilities at the lowest cost without violating the investor's investment policies.

Thus, while the theory behind a cash-flow matching portfolio is simple and straightforward, the practice of actually building a cash-flow matched portfolio can be very complex.

**Immunized Portfolios.** Another way to fund a specific liability stream is with an *immunized portfolio*. An immunized portfolio is one with a weighted duration equal to the investment horizon. When there are multiple liabilities (as in our example), we would buy a portfolio for each liability whose duration matched the time horizon of the liability. Thus we would buy bonds with a duration of 1 year, 2 years, and so on to match our 1-year, 2-year, and so on liabilities.

Because our portfolio's durations are equal to the time horizons of our liabilities, the interest-rate risk and reinvestment risk to which we are exposed should (approximately) be offsetting. Thus if market interest rates rise and the market value of our securities declines, the decline should be offset by an approximately equal increase in the amount of IOI. On the other hand, if market interest rates decline, the amount of IOI earned will be lower, but the lower IOI should be offset by an increase in the market value of our bonds.

By matching durations and liabilities, we are able to buy longer-term bonds than we could with either a dedicated portfolio or a cash-matching portfolio. Assuming the yield curve is positively sloped, the longer the weighted average life of our portfolio, the higher our weighted average yield will be.

Thus a properly constructed immunized portfolio should have a higher average yield than either a dedicated portfolio or a cash-flow matching portfolio *on the day each is established.* Unfortunately, this is not the only consideration in determining the relative cost of these various options.

While a dedicated and a cash-flow portfolio can be left virtually undisturbed after they are bought, this is not the case for an immunized portfolio. An immunized portfolio has to be periodically *rebalanced*, meaning that periodically, the bonds in the portfolio need to be replaced with different bonds whose durations more closely match the time horizon of the liabilities. This is necessary because a given bond's duration changes over time.

As time passes, the time horizons of the liabilities shorten, as do the durations of the bonds. Unfortunately, the liabilities and the durations grow shorter at different rates. Thus the more time that passes, the more misaligned the bond's duration becomes with the time horizons of the liabilities. Therefore new bonds, with durations more closely matching the new time frames of the liabilities, must be periodically purchased. The old bonds, whose durations no longer match the time frames of the liabilities, must be sold.

The more frequently a portfolio is rebalanced, the more likely it is to generate cash flows that exactly match the liabilities. Unfortunately, portfolio managers cannot buy and sell bonds for nothing. There are transaction costs that include the spread between the bid and asked prices, the commissions charged, and the cost of time and effort spent rebalancing the portfolio. So the more frequently a portfolio is rebalanced, the more immunized it will be but the higher the transaction costs will also be.

Managers of immunized portfolios must make a choice between maintaining an exact balance in their portfolios and limiting their transaction costs. Most managers compromise and only rebalance their portfolios every six months or so. Thus most immunized portfolios are allowed to get slightly out of balance in order to save transaction costs.

Another factor in determining the frequency with which an immunized portfolio needs to be rebalanced is the frequency and magnitude of swings in the market interest rate. The greater the magnitude and frequency of changes in market interest rates, the more frequently an immunized portfolio needs to be rebalanced.

In effect, then, in immunizing a portfolio, a manager tries to keep two moving targets (durations and liabilities) matched. If this match is maintained, the probability is very high that the cash flows generated by the portfolio will be sufficient to meet the liability schedule. In exchange for this high probability of success, the investor accepts a lower yield than the yields of active management but a higher yield than either a dedicated or cash-flow matched portfolio would return.

**Passive Management Without Liability Matching.** If an investor is not trying to match a specific liability schedule, he or she will use different passive-management strategies.

**Ladder Portfolios.** A *ladder portfolio* is a portfolio where bonds are scheduled to mature in a proportional, sequential pattern. For ex-

*Table 13-2.* The Maturity Schedule of a Ladder Portfolio.

| No. of Years to Maturity | Face Amount |
|:---:|:---:|
| 2 | $5000 |
| 4 | 5000 |
| 6 | 5000 |
| 8 | 5000 |
| 10 | 5000 |
| 12 | 5000 |
| 14 | 5000 |
| 16 | 5000 |
| 18 | 5000 |
| 20 | 5000 |

ample, if an investor wants to put $100,000 in the bond market but does not want to actively manage the portfolio, the investor might buy bonds with the maturity schedule shown in Table 13-2 above. In this portfolio, $5,000 matures every two years over a 20-year period. Each of the principal payments is then reinvested in bonds that mature 20 years later, perpetuating the ladder ad infinitum. Under this strategy, the investor is always reinvesting the principal received at the *then* current market interest rate.

This approach is very appealing to investors who have little confidence in active management and want to implement a *simple* strategy that will, *over time*, generate a return approximately equal to the market's return.

**Index Portfolios.** Another passive strategy is building a portfolio that mirrors the performance of a specified universe of bonds. For example, a manager might want to build a portfolio that will *always* perform as well (or as poorly) as the bond market as a whole. This is more difficult than it seems.

In order to *exactly* mirror the performance of the entire bond market, the investor has to buy a weighted average of every bond available in the marketplace. Since this is too ludicrous to consider, we are obviously going to have to sacrifice exactly mirroring the market for the sake of practicality.

The question is, how many different bond issues do we need to invest in in order to reasonably mirror the performance of the market? We know that one issue would have only a very slight probability of mirroring the market's performance, while buying every issue would give us a 100% probability of mirroring performance.

Fortunately, it is now widely believed that a given universe of bonds can be reasonably approximated by a carefully selected portfolio of 40 to 50 different bond issues. Thus, by investing a weighted proportion of our portfolio into 40 or 50 carefully selected issues, we can accurately and predictably mirror the performance of the entire bond market.

For narrower universes (i.e., the Treasury-bond market, the AAA-rated corporate-bond market, and so on), the number of issues we need to buy is even smaller.

The type of investor to whom this strategy appeals is the investor who has, in the past, hired bond-portfolio managers to actively manage a bond portfolio and ended up paying high management fees for performance that underperformed the market as a whole (or a more directly comparable subuniverse). In disgust, the investor elects to pay a minimal management fee in order to have a return with a high probability of matching the market's performance.

## Active Management

Investors who are less callous (or who have not yet been burned by an active bond manager) may also elect to actively manage their bond portfolios. Active managers make educated guesses about the future direction of interest rates, changes in credit ratings, effects of future legislation, and so on. If they're right, their portfolios will outperform a comparable passive portfolio.

Regardless of how many factors the investor takes into consideration when adjusting the portfolio, the most important factor is still the change in future market interest rates. Because no one (to date) has been able to predict future interest rates accurately, academics still debate whether anyone can significantly outperform the market over long periods of time.

# INDEX

## A

"Absolute" return, 20–21
Accrued interest
  calculating, 56–59
  definition, 56
  effect of, on yield, 60
  settlement and, 55–60
Active management of portfolio, 166–67
  definition, 157
Adjustable-rate mortgage (ARM), 103
Adjustable-rate securities, 13
Adjustment of floater, frequency of, 143–44
Amortization in early years and approach of maturity, 20
Amortization schedule of $200,000, 10% 30-year mortgage, 109, 110–19
Annualized return of stock investment and choice of CB, 97–98
Annuities, 160
ARM (Adjustable-rate mortgage), 103
Asked price and bid price, spread between, 2
Average-life approximations, of sinking-fund bonds, 75–76

## B

Basis points, 2
Bid price and asked price, spread between, 2
Bond(s)
  adjustable-rate, 13
  callable, 61–63
    called per year, percentage of, 72
    zeros, 92
  convertible, *see* Convertible bonds
  corporate, 1–2; *see also* Corporate bonds
  coupon, 89–92
  definition, 11
  discount, 63–64
  exchangeable, 93
  floating-rate, *see* Floating-rate bonds

repurchasing, 69–70
  similar, definition, 37
  sinking-fund, 67–76
  symmetrical, 146–47
  tail, 92
  U.S. government, 2, 58–59, 90, 91
  volatility of, *see* Volatility of bond
  zero-coupon, *see* Zero-coupon bonds
Bondswaps, 151–55
  floating-rate securities and, 150
  types of
    credit, 153
    objectives, 155
    rate-anticipation, 151–52
    sector, 153–54
    substitution, 152–53
    tax, 154–55
Business days, definition, 55
Buying and selling zeros, 88–89
Buying power of interest and IOI payments and principal, 30

## C

Call, partial, 62
Call protection, 61–62
Call provisions, 61 63
  definition, 13
  discount bonds and, 63–64
  of floater, and put provisions, 145
Callable bonds, 61–63
  zeros, 92
Calls and puts, effect of, on yield, 61–66
Cash flow
  compounding of interest and, 5
  for 15-year, 10% bond, 22
    reinvestment rates and, 25–29
  of net-net-realized compound yield, 28–29
  for simple interest loan, 4
Cash-flow matching, 160–62
CBs, *see* Convertible bonds
CMOs, *see* Collateralized Mortgage Obligations

## Z